The Reluctant

A Play

William Douglas Home

Samuel French – London
New York – Sydney – Toronto – Hollywood

PRODUCTION NOTE

The Scene. This should be intimate, not deep and with a corner of the kitchen through door down R. and a corner of the hall through door L.C. in view, should give the feeling of a not very large flat. In the colouring and décor it is as well to remember that it is an apartment rented for some three months or so and, while pleasant-looking, probably does not reflect the taste of the present tenants. A large window occupying most of the L. wall gives an opportunity for plenty of sunlight in Act 1, Scene 1 and Act 2, Scene 2, for it is summer-time in a gay season. In Act 1, Scene 2 the lights come on on Sheila Broadbent's entrance in evening dress after a very slow fade and are on again from the Broadbents' return at the opening of Act 2, Scene 1. Main switch by door L.C.

The less the characters are acted, the better. They are real people in a quite real situation, and the less effort made the better will it all come off. Sheila Broadbent has the hardest task, for the telephone conversations are quite a hurdle, and the actress playing her should be careful always to remember that there is someone—indeed, a variety of persons—at the other end of the line. Moreover, the first scene depends largely on her making it continuously surprising and interesting. Jimmy returns later in the play to reap the benefit of the atmosphere of enjoyment thus engendered.

The play is so full of laughs that some are expendable. The players should not worry about them *all*. Be a little thrifty in this respect.

Future David Bullochs should be careful to eschew all thought of breadth. Do not try to be funny. The part is funny enough. Be real. Clarissa and Mabel Crosswaite are merely another mother and daughter with the same end in view, namely, the marriage market, only their approach to the matter in hand is different. Jane Broadbent need not fear to be a little nicely rude. She's young and was of the impression that she did not want any part of the boring business; that it was all going to be a nuisance and no good could come of it. In fact, magic came of it. She should never be "knowing" and when in doubt should go for absolute simplicity. Jimmy needs only to be an amusing personality and should never try to be funny nor to add anything more than is called for. The scene between father and daughter in the second Act should be delicately handled and played for what it is worth, which is a little more than merely laughs. Hoylake-Johnston should have presence, poise and gentleness.

When we were first rehearsing the play, the author pointed out that in writing the dialogue he had intended a certain rhythm—a beat—and this is by no means as unlikely as might appear at first glance, as no doubt will be seen by good players.

Lastly, the director should not be afraid to get the play spanking along at a good pace. The audience have to be controlled and disciplined and must not be allowed to hold up the action, or no one will get home. The whole evening is one of fun, but controlled fun; and no one, the players or the audience, must get out of hand.

The curtain to Act 1, Scene 1 should be medium-slow, Scene 2 quick. Those to Act 2 should be slow.

JACK MINSTER

TO MY WIFE

The Reluctant Debutante

This play was first presented by E. P. Clift in conjunction with **Anna Deere Wiman** at The Cambridge Theatre, London, on 24th May, 1955, with the following cast of characters:

JIMMY BROADBENT	*Wilfrid Hyde White*
SHEILA BROADBENT (his wife)	*Celia Johnson*
JANE (his daughter)	*Anna Massey*
MABEL CROSSWAITE	*Ambrosine Phillpotts*
CLARISSA (her daughter)	*Anna Steele*
DAVID BULLOCH	*Peter Myers*
DAVID HOYLAKE-JOHNSTON	*John Merivale*
MRS. EDGAR	*Gwynne Whitby*

Directed by JACK MINSTER

Setting by HUTCHINSON SCOTT

The scene is laid throughout in JIMMY BROADBENT's flat, off Eaton Square, in June.

ACT ONE

SCENE 1.   Breakfast time.
SCENE 2.   Cocktail time, the same evening.

ACT TWO

SCENE 1.   Early the following morning.
SCENE 2.   Breakfast time.

NOTE: *Running time of this play, excluding interval, is approximately two hours.*

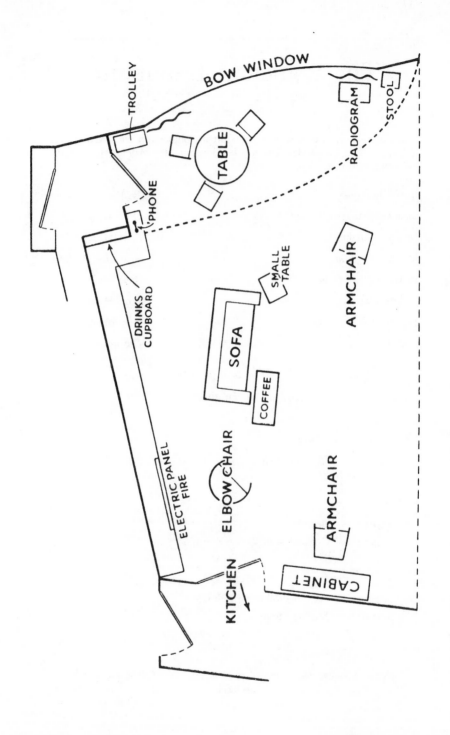

THE RELUCTANT DEBUTANTE

ACT ONE

Scene i

The scene is laid throughout in the sitting-room of the Broadbents' *flat in London. This flat, which has been rented for the London season, is clearly not their home.*

Through a window on the left can be seen roof-tops. On r., *a service door leads into the kitchen. Back-stage* l.c. *is the sitting-room door, leading into the passage, in which all doors, bathroom, bedroom, cupboard, etc., are situated.*

Jimmy l. *and* Sheila Broadbent l.c., *are seated at breakfast.* Sheila *is opening letters.*

Sheila (*opening a letter*). Lord and Lady Aspath. Who on earth are they? July the seventh. The Hyde Park Hotel. (*She puts it down and opens another.*) Mrs. Arthur Milligan. I've never heard of her.

(Jimmy *covers his plate with his side plate.*)
What is the matter, darling?

Jimmy. My poached egg . . .

Sheila. What's wrong with it?

Jimmy. I just don't like the way it's looking at me.

Sheila. Well, drink your orange juice.

Jimmy. I can't. It lowers my morale.

Sheila. Well, have some coffee, then.

Jimmy. That's not a bad idea. (*Rises and crosses to trolley.*) I don't know how you do it, darling. You look marvellous, considering we weren't in till three.

(Sheila *rises with two envelopes, crosses to wastepaper basket behind sofa and tears up the envelopes.*)

Sheila. Give me some, too. What were you drinking last night, Jimmy?

Jimmy. Anything that I could lay my hands on: champagne, whisky, cigarette ash, lipstick, lemonade . . .

Sheila. Why can't you stick to one thing or the other?

Jimmy (*pouring* Sheila *a cup of coffee*). Well, the thing that I was sticking

to ran out. So I went over to the other, until that ran out as well.
And then I had to scavenge round among the empties.

SHEILA. Don't . . .

JIMMY. I'm sorry, darling, but you asked. Bring me *The Times* will
you?

(SHEILA *collects* The Times *from back of sofa.*)

SHEILA. We mustn't let that happen at our dance.

JIMMY (*pouring out his coffee*). It's bound to, if I'm going to keep awake.

(SHEILA *returns to table and sits.*)

SHEILA. No, darling, I'm not talking about you. We must lay in an
adequate supply of drink.

JIMMY (*returning coffee pot and milk jug to trolley*). Don't worry about
that: I'll lay on everything from vodka down to hashish; I'm
aiming at complete unconsciousness.

SHEILA. Jimmy, it's on the thirtieth. Three weeks, Jimmy. Oh!
Isn't it exciting? Only three weeks, Jimmy!

JIMMY (*sits at table*). Only three? I doubt if I'll live to see it.

SHEILA. Don't be silly, darling.

JIMMY. I'm not being silly. This damned racket's killing me. In three
weeks I'll be nothing but a walking ulcer in full evening dress.

SHEILA. Well, anyway, it's bringing lots of invitations in for Jane.

JIMMY. What is—my ulcer?

SHEILA. No, our dance.

JIMMY. Oh, good! Let's have it on my tombstone: "By his Death,
My Much Beloved Husband Brought a Lot of Invitations in for
Jane".

SHEILA. Now, Lord and Lady Aspath: who are they?

JIMMY. Why?

SHEILA. Well, they've asked us to a dance.

JIMMY. Well, he was Bobby Nicholson before his father became a
peer.

SHEILA. Why did he get a peerage?

JIMMY. Long time ago. The river Itchen ran through his garden,
and the Prime Minister was fond of fishing. Something of that sort.

SHEILA. And who was she?

JIMMY. Oh, London-Irish.

SHEILA. What on earth is that?

JIMMY. She worked in poor old Florrie's night club.

SHEILA. Oh yes, I know who you mean. She waved to me last week
at Newmarket. She looked simply sweet.

JIMMY. She is sweet, so they say.

SHEILA. The dance is for their daughter, Mary Anne; I wonder what she's like?

JIMMY. I hope she's like her mother, for her sake. I was at school with Bobby Nicholson. Do you know, I saw him the other day at Black's and he looked exactly the same as he did his first term at Ludgrove, except that he had trousers on instead of shorts?

SHEILA. Well, as we know them both, I think we must accept. We owe it to our darling Jane.

(SHEILA *picks up another invitation as* JIMMY *returns to* The Times.)

SHEILA. Now Mrs. Arthur Milligan. Who's she, Jimmy? Jimmy!

JIMMY. I'm reading about Mr. Nehru, darling.

SHEILA. You can do that in the office. Pay attention, now. Who's Mrs. Arthur Milligan?

JIMMY. I've never heard of her.

SHEILA. Oh dear, I haven't either. Ought we to accept it?

JIMMY. What's it for?

SHEILA. A dance—the twenty-eighth.

JIMMY. Where?

SHEILA. River Room. Savoy.

JIMMY. That sounds all right.

SHEILA. What does?

JIMMY. Well, the address. It might have been the Albert Hall.

SHEILA. But darling, what about her husband?

JIMMY. What about him?

SHEILA. He's not on the invitation card.

JIMMY. Perhaps she hasn't got one.

SHEILA. But she must have one. The daughter's called Belinda.

JIMMY. That's no proof she's got a husband.

SHEILA. But she must have had one some time, Jimmy.

JIMMY. Perhaps he's dead.

SHEILA. Oh what a good idea. I never thought of that. I'll say "Yes" on the understanding that he's dead. We owe it to our darling Jane. Oh, here's another one. (*Reading.*) The Duke and Duchess of . . . Good heavens, what's come over Sylvia? Oh no, it's only cocktails. I was going to say if Sylvia's persuaded Tom to give a party for those horse-faced girls, she ought to get a medal. But she hasn't. It's just cocktails. Well, she'll never get them off on gin.

(*She gets up to put the cards on the mantelpiece.*) It's a disgrace. (*Picks up notebook and pencil.*)

JIMMY. What is?

SHEILA. Tom's attitude. He's as rich as Croesus and he's won the Derby twice, and he won't lift a finger for those wretched girls.

JIMMY. He should have run them in the Oaks.

SHEILA. Well anyway, that's two more. (D.S. *with notebook, after tearing up last envelope.*)

JIMMY. How many nights of purgatory does that add up to?

SHEILA. Thirty-one.

JIMMY. How many of 'em do we know?

SHEILA. Sixteen.

JIMMY. That's not a bad percentage in these days.

SHEILA. It'll be thirty-two, with ours.

JIMMY. Don't Sheila, don't!

SHEILA. You don't think people will be bored with the River Room by the thirtieth? I mean, if they've just been there on the twenty-eighth?

JIMMY. I hope so.

SHEILA. Jimmy! We're giving it for dearest Jane.

JIMMY. And dearest Mary Ann. And dearest Mrs. Arthur Milligan, and all the dearest debutantes in London. You're telling me they're dearest. They're so damned dear they're going to cost me fifteen hundred pounds. And all for what? Eleven-thirty until four-thirty—five interminable hours at three hundred an hour! What's that a minute? Knock off a nought. Six into thirty. What's that, darling?

SHEILA. Oh, I shouldn't think it's very much!

JIMMY. It's five. Five pounds a minute.

SHEILA. Well, put it down to entertainment, Jimmy.

JIMMY. Entertainment!

SHEILA (*crosses back to table and sits*). What a good idea! He's so nice, your accountant, if you took him out to lunch occasionally—

JIMMY. He's not as nice as that, my dear. If he was only half that nice he'd find himself in Wormwood Scrubs.

SHEILA. Well, business. I'm sure it's business.

JIMMY. It's that all right. But I'm afraid the Inland Revenue are still sufficiently romantic about marriage to regard it as an institution rather than a business.

SHEILA. An institution—well, let's call it that. Like military service is for men.

JIMMY (*rises to door* L. *back*). It doesn't matter what you call it, darling. It's a bloody menace.

SHEILA. Well, it's only going to happen once.

JIMMY (*going out to bedroom for coat*). Thank goodness for that. Five pounds a minute! All for what?

SHEILA. I've told you, dear. For Jane.

JIMMY (*off*). She isn't worth it. No one is.

SHEILA. Of course she is. Let's work it out. (*Rises and crosses to* R. *of door.*) What does she cost to keep?

JIMMY (*off*). Five hundred a year.

SHEILA. Well, there you are. Five hundred into fifteen hundred. That's three. In three years' time, if Jane's not married you'd be out of pocket, if you see what I mean. Do you see what I mean?

JIMMY (*re-enters*). Yes. Do you?

SHEILA. No, but I did a minute ago.

JIMMY. Well, what you mean is based on sand. You're arguing on the assumption that giving a Deb dance for Jane will get Jane married.

SHEILA. It might.

JIMMY (*closes door*). And it might not.

SHEILA. Well, even if it doesn't, it's our "thank-you" for the other dances.

JIMMY (*puts paper on back of sofa, collects spectacles' cleaning-stuff from shelf*). An expensive thank you, thank you very much.

SHEILA. Please, not all that again. It's not only a "thank you" for the other dances, it's a "thank you" for the whole season (*Crosses back to table and sits.*) during which Jane has been given the chance to meet lots of nice young men, one of whom may marry her.

JIMMY. Good—well, let's hope one of 'em does.

SHEILA. Oh, Jimmy, don't you think one will?

JIMMY. I wouldn't be surprised. She's not repulsive. (*Cleaning glasses* C. *behind sofa.*)

SHEILA. Isn't she? Oh, Jimmy, isn't she?

JIMMY (*crossing towards her*). You sound as if you thought she was.

SHEILA. I just can't judge. I've seen too much of her.

JIMMY. No more than I have.

SHEILA. No, but you're a man. And you'd know.

JIMMY (*pulling her leg*). Well . . . I'd say she was attractive—like her mother.

SHEILA. Thank you, darling . . .

(He gives her a kiss.)

JIMMY (*crosses below sofa*). What's the orders for tonight?

SHEILA. Drinks, sevenish. And, as we're dressing, please don't hang about in Black's.

JIMMY. Who's coming?

SHEILA. Mabel and Clarissa.

JIMMY. Not those spots!

SHEILA. She isn't spotty any more. At least, not superficially.

JIMMY (*returns glasses' cleaning-material to shelf*). Oh, good. Why dress?

SHEILA. Because we're dining out.

JIMMY. With them?

SHEILA. No. Just ourselves and Jane. We've got to go to Rhoda Gregson's dance.

JIMMY. Oh Lord, I haven't slept since Sunday night!

SHEILA. I know, my darling. But you mustn't give in now.

JIMMY (*below sofa*). What number is tonight?

SHEILA. Nineteen.

JIMMY. That's thirteen more to go. I used to keep a calendar at school. I haven't got the nerve to now. Where shall we dine?

SHEILA. Oh, anywhere.

JIMMY (*crossing towards door*). I'll get Miss Grey to get a table somewhere.

SHEILA. Yes.

JIMMY. How many? Three or four?

SHEILA. Three, I'm afraid.

JIMMY. What? No young man?

SHEILA. No. Are you in a dreadful hurry, Jimmy?

JIMMY (*at door, about to go out*). Yes.

SHEILA. Well then, sit down a minute. I'm extremely worried about Jane. I've got to tell you, Jimmy.

JIMMY. Why, what's wrong?

SHEILA (*rises and crosses to telephone*). You won't believe me, but I've literally been hanging on that telephone for weeks.

JIMMY. I will. I got the bill this morning. (*Crosses to table and picks up bill.*)

SHEILA (*behind sofa*). Nobody'll come. But nobody. I went down Rhoda Gregson's list from A to Z—and not one single solitary man will come and dine tonight. There must be something wrong with Jane.

JIMMY (*crossing below sofa to brief-case in* U.R. *chair*). There may be something wrong with Rhoda Gregson's list.

SHEILA. Of course there isn't, Jimmy! (*Crossing round below* D.S. *arm of sofa.*) Everybody's on it. Everybody. No, Rhoda Gregson's list's all right. It's Jane. She isn't any good with men. She doesn't know any. She doesn't want to know any.

JIMMY. Wise girl!

SHEILA. No, Jimmy. It's not funny. No, it's not. It's very, very worrying. You've got to talk to her.

JIMMY. Me? Why on earth should I?

SHEILA (*crossing* R.). Well, you're a man—you can tell her what the young men want.

JIMMY. My dear!

SHEILA. Now, don't be silly, but of course you can. You were a young man once. And you can tell her what the young men want. I'm sure they don't change much.

JIMMY (*sits* U.S. *end of coffee table*). You bet they don't!

SHEILA (*behind him*). Well, will you talk to her?

JIMMY. No, I will not.

SHEILA. Oh darling, don't be selfish! Surely you could do just that! I watched her all last night. Where were we?

JIMMY. River Room.

SHEILA. Well, she was terrible.

JIMMY. I never noticed anything.

SHEILA. Of course, you didn't notice anything. You stood there by the bar for three hours and talked to all your men friends. (*Crosses* D.R. *and sits in chair below door, rubbing feet.*) I do think you might have had the grace to introduce her to a few young men.

JIMMY. I don't know any.

SHEILA. Well, a few old men.

JIMMY. You told me not to when I did the other night.

SHEILA. Well, he's notorious.

JIMMY. I don't know any young men, Sheila. All the men I know are middle-aged and don't like dancing. Anyway, I went round with her twice myself. Well, give me that, at least!

SHEILA. I saw you. And what happened? She came limping back the first time with her shoestrap broken, and one stocking laddered. And the second time you missed her feet completely and just tore her shoulder-strap.

JIMMY. I think you're overtired. You should have stayed in bed.

SHEILA (*rises to* U.S. *behind* JIMMY *to above sofa*). I can't. I've got to get a man for dinner, if it kills me.

JIMMY. Why not hire a gigolo?

SHEILA. I doubt if I could find one.

JIMMY. Shall I get Miss Grey to try and trace one?

SHEILA. Jimmy, don't be silly. Everyone at Rhoda Gregson's dance would know that he was one. Jimmy, it's so worrying! She may turn out like your Aunt Eileen, living in a flat in Gloucester Gate with a bull terrier. (*Below* D.S. *end of sofa.*)

JIMMY. Darling! Aunt Eileen's eighty-two. Jane's seventeen. That gives her sixty-five years weight for age. I wouldn't let it get you down quite yet, if I were you.

SHEILA. But she's exactly like that photograph of your Aunt Eileen playing croquet in your mother's book.

JIMMY. No one could be quite like that photograph. Not even my Aunt Eileen. (*Rises to shelf for cigarettes to fill cigarette case.*)

SHEILA. And Jane loves animals.

JIMMY. Yes, horses. But I doubt if she'd be allowed to set up house with one in Gloucester Gate.

SHEILA (*crossing below breakfast table to* U.S. *window*). And dogs. (*Opens* U.S. *window.*)

JIMMY. Darling, everybody loves dogs, but it doesn't stop them marrying—the people or the dogs. Now don't be silly, darling. I thought Jane was doing pretty well last night.

SHEILA (*to* D.S. *of table*). Oh yes. She danced with lots of people. Once.

JIMMY. Well, why not ask one of them?

SHEILA. I did. I asked them all when they had finished with her. No, I didn't. I missed one. I'll run and ask her who he was. (*Starts towards the door.*) Yes, I remember perfectly. He went off somewhere when they finished dancing, and just left her standing there. (*Calling through the door.* JIMMY *crosses to mirror below kitchen door and looks at himself.*) Jane darling—Jane, are you awake?

JANE (*off*). Yes.

SHEILA. Where are you? Oh, Jane, who was that young man you danced the fox trot with?

JANE (*off*). Which, Mummy?

SHEILA. Darling, that's exactly what I'm asking you.

JANE (*off*). Which fox trot, Mummy?

SHEILA. The one where Lady Price fell down.

JANE (*off*). Oh, David.

SHEILA. David who?

JANE (*off*). I wouldn't know.

SHEILA (*returning*). She really is too casual for words! (U.R. *behind sofa*.) Imagine dancing with a total stranger and not asking what his name is . . .

(JANE *comes in in dressing gown*.)

JANE. What's the flap for, Mummy? Hello, Daddy. (*Crosses to him and kisses him*.)

JIMMY. Hallo.

SHEILA. Jane, who introduced you to this David?

JANE. Daddy.

JIMMY. Me, Jane? When?

JANE. When you were dancing with me.

SHEILA. What's he look like?

JANE. Goofy. (*Kisses* SHEILA.)

JIMMY. I know who she means. There was a fellow dancing alongside us, so I introduced her.

SHEILA. Did you know him?

JIMMY. Not from Adam! I just did it out of bonhomie. He didn't seem to mind!

(JANE *looks at new invitations on shelf*.)

SHEILA. Who was he dancing with?

JIMMY. The girl we talked about just now, who isn't spotty any more.

SHEILA. Clarissa!

JIMMY. That's right—Mabel's girl.

SHEILA. Well, let's get on to Mabel now; she's sure to know. Now what's her number?

JIMMY. Don't ask me, my dear! (*Crosses below sofa to breakfast table, picks up some letters and puts them in his brief-case*.)

SHEILA. Jane darling, who's Aunt Mabel under now?

JANE. Sir Charles Munro.

JIMMY. Jane!

JANE. What's the matter, Daddy?

JIMMY. Well . . .

SHEILA (*telephone book in hand*). That's right—she took his flat last winter when he went to Paris. (*Puts telephone book on back of sofa*.) M for Mountjoy, Munro, Murgatroyd . . . oh dear, I've jumped it. M-U-N . . . (JIMMY *removes* The Times *from under telephone directory*) yes, here we are. Munro, Sir Charles. Sloane 7381.

JIMMY. Well, I must go. See you tonight. (*Exit* U.L.C.)

SHEILA. Oh darling, please don't interrupt. Jane dear, what did I say?

JANE. Sloane 7381.

(SHEILA *dials*.)

SHEILA. Good-bye, darling. And don't be late. Remember about
Mabel . . .

JANE (*crossing below sofa to breakfast table*). Mummy . . .

SHEILA. Yes, what is it, darling?

JANE. Daddy's gone.

SHEILA. Yes, darling, I expect he has. Why, did you want him?

JANE. No, but couldn't you stop talking to him when he isn't here?

(JANE *drinks orange juice and glances at two letters which she
opens.*)

SHEILA (*on telephone*). Hullo? Mabel? Darling, yes, it is. Mabel
darling. Tell me, who was that young man Clarissa danced the
fox trot with last night? Which one? Well, the one where Lady
Price fell down. I know, my dear—poor Harold really ought to
keep an eye on her. I know. Too dangerous for words. My dear
—and did you see the French Ambassador? He had to literally
hurdle her, with Eileen Privett in his arms. I know—and she's no
midget, is she? Yes, poor man, I do hope that he hasn't strained his
heart. (JANE *crosses to trolley.*) Well, Mabel, what did I ring up
about? Oh yes, of course—Jane says his name is David. I don't
know. I'll ask her. (*To* JANE.) Darling, Mabel says do you mean
David Bulloch?

JANE. Ask her if he's goofy-looking.

SHEILA (*at telephone*). Jane says is he goofy-looking? (*To* JANE.) Yes, a
little, dear. (*At telephone.*) No, no, of course it doesn't matter. Do
you know where I could get hold of him? Yes, please do, Mabel—
that's too kind of you. (*To* JANE.) She's sent Clarissa up to get her
book. (*At telephone.*) Yes, wasn't it too lovely! Did you? Oh,
how sweet of you. I simply must tell her at once. I know she'll be
thrilled. (*To* JANE, *who is leaving trolley with a plate of scrambled egg.*)
Jane darling, Mabel says you looked too wonderful for words last
night.

(JANE, *at* U.S.R. *end of table, puts out her tongue.*)

(*At telephone.*) She's thrilled. And what about Clarissa? Did she
like it? I'm so glad. I thought that she was looking simply radiant.
(JANE *sits at* D.S. *place.*) She is so sensible not dancing all the time.
Oh, has she? . . . Oh, I see, her shoe's been rubbing her—poor
thing! Oh, Mabel, by the way, who was that very dark young man
Clarissa danced a waltz with? Sunburn, was it? David Hoylake-
Johnston. Where's he come from? Oh, two years. The lucky boy.

I always think Majorca's too divine. Oh, Malaya!—poor dear boy—
Not so dear! But what do you mean, Mabel? If he's not all right,
why ever did you let Clarissa dance with him? (JANE *rises*, U.S. *to
trolley with cup and saucer. Inspects coffee and milk jug.*) No—I suppose
you couldn't, if they met at dinner. No—no—Mabel—no! (*To*
JANE.) Jane—run into the kitchen and ask Mrs. Edgar for some more
hot milk.

JANE. There's lots here.

SHEILA. It's cold surely, darling.

JANE (*pouring out the milk*). That won't matter. There's no coffee left.

SHEILA (*puts down cup, picks up coffee pot*). Jane, do as you're told.

(JANE *goes out* U.L.C. *with coffee pot.*)

(*Brings telephone* D.S.) Yes, Mabel, do go on. I've sent Jane to the
kitchen. Oh, my dear—so that's why Brenda Barrington went off
to ski in May. He was the man. But didn't you just say that he was
in Malaya? Oh, I see—his leave had started then. I know, my dear.
That always seems to make them so impetuous.

(JANE *returns with coffee pot.*)

(*At telephone.*) Well, Mabel, till tonight, and you must tell me all.
(*She hangs up and replaces telephone* U.S.) Oh bother. I haven't got
the number now!

(JANE *pours coffee into her cup and replaces the jug on trolley.*)

JANE. It serves you right. You shouldn't gossip so.

SHEILA. But, darling, I was doing it for you.

JANE. I don't want David Bulloch for a partner, thank you. (*Sits* U.S.
place with cup.)

SHEILA. Why not, darling? (C.) Mabel says he's charming.

JANE. Everybody knows he's goofy.

SHEILA. Nonsense, Jane. Now. What was Mabel's number?

JANE. I've forgotten.

(SHEILA *goes to telephone book on back of sofa and looks it up
again.*)

You're only asking him because he's going to be a peer.

SHEILA. A what?

JANE. A peer. You know what peers are, Mummy. David's going to
be Lord Cirencester.

SHEILA (*feigning ignorance*). Who told you, Jane?

JANE. He did.

SHEILA. How very vulgar he must be.

JANE. Well, it's no more than someone saying he's going to be an engine driver.

SHEILA. No one ever says that, darling.

JANE. I expect engine drivers do.

SHEILA. When they've been asked, perhaps. I hope you didn't ask him, darling.

JANE. No, he told me straight out of the blue—just like you might say, "Jane is coming out this year," he said, "I'll be Lord Cirencester one day actually".

SHEILA. And what did you say?

JANE. Oh, I said it couldn't bore me more.

SHEILA. How very rude.

JANE. He quite agreed. He said it couldn't bore me more than it bored him.

SHEILA (*she has found the number*). Oh, did he, darling? He sounds fun. Sloane 7381. (U.S. *to telephone.*) We really ought to write it down somewhere. (*She dials.*)

JANE. I can't see why.

SHEILA. Well, darling, after all, Clarissa is your greatest friend.

JANE. She's not.

SHEILA. Of course she is.

JANE. She's all right in the country, but she's horrible in London.

SHEILA. Horrible? Of course she isn't.

JANE. Yes, she is. She's always giggling and looking sideways.

SHEILA. Nonsense, darling. That's just your imagination.

JANE. No, it's not. It's hers.

SHEILA. Engaged. (*She replaces the receiver and then crosses* D.S. *and sits in chair* D.R.C.) Did you like any of the young men that you danced with last night, darling?

JANE. No.

SHEILA. You must have found some of them nicer than the others?

JANE. No, I didn't. They were all the same.

SHEILA. Darling, how absurd, no two people are the same!

JANE. They are.

SHEILA. What did they talk to you about?

JANE. Oh, Ascot, Wimbledon and Goodwood. And the dance the night before, and then the dance the next night. It's so boring I could scream.

SHEILA. But you like dancing, don't you?

JANE. Not with them.

SHEILA. Why not?

JANE. They're all so young.

SHEILA. You mean they don't dance properly?

JANE. Oh yes, they do. That's just what's wrong. They couldn't dance more properly.

SHEILA. Darling, what do you mean?

JANE. Oh, Mummy, you know quite well what I mean. They dance just like two people going for a walk, except that *you're* walking backwards. Well, that's not what dancing's for. I mean, when natives dance a love dance out in Africa, it means something.

SHEILA. Oh! What does it mean, darling?

JANE. Well, they're making love.

SHEILA. Jane!

JANE. I don't mean literally. It's in the early stages still.

SHEILA (*relieved*). Oh.

JANE. But they're hotting up for it. That's why they do it. Otherwise they wouldn't do it. They'd go out for a walk instead.

SHEILA. But, darling, they're primitive!

JANE. Well, love is primitive.

SHEILA. Oh, is it, darling?

JANE. That's just what I like about them. They're honest and we aren't. They know what dancing's for. And if it's not for that, it's not for anything.

(SHEILA *laughs*.)

What are you laughing at?

SHEILA. Oh, nothing. (*She laughs again.*) I just had a vision of your father bounding up and down in feathers in the River Room.

JANE. Well, it'd do him much more good than propping up the bar all night.

SHEILA. There I agree.

JANE. I knew you would.

SHEILA. Only about Daddy, darling. I still disagree in principle. I must try Mabel for that young man's number now. (*She gets to the telephone again.*) Just think! I danced with two M.P.s last night, one Minister, two Colonels and the Air Attaché from the Swedish Embassy. Well, if one only danced as a preliminary to making love, my goodness! I wouldn't have much reputation left this morning, would I? (*She has got through at last and takes telephone round* U.S. *end of sofa and sits on sofa.*) Oh, Mabel, darling, we were cut off. It's too annoying, isn't it? Now, Mabel, did Clarissa get the . . . Oh, how kind of you! (*To* JANE.) Write it down. And stop picking your nose. (*At telephone.*) No, Mabel, don't be silly. I was talking to Jane. You were, too? What a strange coincidence. Yes, yes, I'm ready. (*To* JANE.) Now, darling, write it down. (*In telephone.*) Yes? Mayfair 6384. (*To* JANE.) Thank you so much.

    (JANE *writes it down with a fork on the table cloth.*) What's that? Eileen? In the London Clinic! Strained her what? My dear, I hope the French Ambassador's all right. I just can't wait to hear.

JANE. Gossip—gossip—gossip!

SHEILA (*at telephone*). Mabel darling, keep it till tonight. Good-bye, my darling. (*She hangs up.*) Jane, don't be so rude. She might have heard.

JANE. Well, really, Mummy. It's so boring. (*Rises, crossing below table to radiogram.*) How I wish I was with Tommy!

SHEILA (*lighting up*). Tommy, darling? (*Rises.*) Oh, that horrid horse!

JANE. He isn't horrid, and he never gossips, and he must be getting far too fat. (*Turns on gramophone.*)

SHEILA. Oh, darling, how I wish you weren't quite so fond of animals. It sometimes frightens me.

JANE (*round* U.S. *end of table and sits* U.S. *chair*). You always frighten me. You do. These days—since we came up to London you've changed altogether. You're like, well—you're like the Games Mistress at school—without the games.

SHEILA. Now don't be silly, darling—you're tired.

JANE. Well, whose fault's that? I wanted to come home last night at one, and you refused to let me come till three.

SHEILA. That wasn't my fault, darling.

JANE. Well, whose was it, then?

SHEILA (*crosses to* JANE, *looking over her shoulder*). Your father's. He saw lots of his old friends. Now, come along, that number. Did you write it down?

JANE. Yes.

SHEILA. Really, Jane, on the table cloth. Now what will Mrs. Edgar say? What is that thing, a two or three?

JANE. I don't know, Mummy. I've been picking at it, I'm afraid.

SHEILA. You really are too trying, Jane! I'll try 6284. (*She goes back to the telephone.*)

JANE. I don't know how you've got the nerve to ring him up when you don't know him.

(SHEILA *sits* D.S. *end of sofa and starts dialling.*)

SHEILA. Nonsense, dear. Of course I know him, now I come to think of it. (*Dialling.*) His mother and I came out the same year.

JANE. I'll bet she's dead by now.

SHEILA. Jane! (*At telephone.*) Hullo. Oh, David, is that you? I'm Sheila Broadbent. I'm quite sure you won't remember me. Your mother and I both came out together. What?—I beg your pardon! No—I don't require a taxi, thank you. (*She hangs up.*) Really, Jane, it's all your fault. What did we try that time? 6284?

JANE. Yes.

SHEILA. Then it must be three. (*She redials.*) That man was very rude.

JANE. What did he say?

SHEILA. Never you mind. He almost made me think that I was on the golf-course with your father. Engaged. Oh dear, it's sure to be some beastly woman asking him to dine.

JANE (*rising* C. *with coffee cup*). Oh, Mummy, do relax.

SHEILA (*forgetting the last number*). Darling, what have I been trying?

JANE (*looking at her with interest*). You know, you're perfectly all right at home in the country, Mummy. You behave absolutely normally from morning till night. One wouldn't suspect a thing. Then the moment you come to London you go completely berserk, like a cow when it smells blood.

SHEILA. Of course I can't think why your father and I do all this for you. I really can't. All you deserve is to be left behind to stagnate in the country.

JANE. Can I go back and stagnate then, Mummy?

SHEILA. No, you can't. How can you be so utterly ungrateful, Jane? Your father's taken this flat for you at crushing expense to bring you out and give you every chance. We sit up every night for you until all hours. We both sat up till three last night on your account, and neither of us gets a word of thanks.

JANE. I've told you once, I didn't want to. (*Crosses back to table and replaces coffee cup.*)

SHEILA. I know, don't repeat it. I can't bear it. It just goes to show what an ungrateful little girl you are. Just think how all your country friends are envying you!

JANE. I can't think of one. (*Crossing* U.S. *of sofa takes an apple from bowl of fruit.*)

SHEILA. Of course you can—the Burrell girl.

JANE. Her! She's a Communist.

SHEILA. What nonsense, dear. Her father's our Chief Constable. (*Sits* U.S.R. *chair with feet on coffee table.*)

JANE. I can't help that. She sent a Christmas card to Bulganin* last year.

SHEILA. Well, then, those poor fat creatures at the Vicarage.

JANE. You know they've both gone up to Oxford, Mummy. And what's more, I heard a rumour last week-end that Janet's going steady with a Rugger Blue.

SHEILA. Jane, darling, really! "Going steady"! (*She starts dialling.*)

JANE. Well, as steady as he'll let her. He's South African. His father owns a lot of mines. With diamonds in them.

SHEILA. Money isn't everything.

JANE. I never said it was. I'm only trying to point out that people can get married without passing through the River Room department first. (*Takes a bite from the apple and turns away.*)

SHEILA. Hush, darling. (*She turns to telephone.*) Hullo—is that Mayfair 6384? Oh, at last! Is that you, David? My name's Sheila Broadbent. I'm quite sure you won't remember me—your mother and I both came out together, and I knew you when you were a tiny little boy. Tell me, are you going to Rhoda Gregson's dance tonight? Yes, aren't they boring? I do so agree. Besides, I'm quite sure you're quite flooded out with invitations. Do forget them all, and come and dine with us! It's just a tiny party. Me—my husband, Jimmy Broadbent—I expect you've met him in some of your Clubs—and Jane, our daughter. She's just coming out this year. (*Signs to* JANE *to take her feet off the table.* JANE *doesn't see.*) I think you danced with her last night. Yes, yes—of course there are. How could you possibly remember! Yes, she did. Yes. Every minute of it. Wildly. But, then she's very young. You will! How wonderful! Well, let's say sevenish for seven-thirty. Fourteen Victor Court— you know, just off Sloane Street, the end of Eaton Square. Well, we'll be looking forward to it quite immensely. And we'll have a lovely talk about your mother. By the way, how is she? In the country? How I envy her. Well, when you're telephoning to her next, do give her Sheila's love. Well, good-bye till seven-thirty. (*She hangs up.*) He's coming.

JANE. No, you don't say so!

SHEILA. Charming manners, and a simply charming voice. I've simply

* Or the name of any topical Russian leader.

got to look him up and see exactly who his mother was. (*Rises* U.S. *end of sofa to books.*)

JANE. You mean to say you didn't know her?

SHEILA. Very likely, darling. I'll tell you in a minute. (*She goes for* "*Who's Who*".)

JANE. When's he coming?

SHEILA. Seven-thirty. We'll all go out. Oh dear, I'll have to telephone to Jimmy now about the table. Will he be there yet? (*Picking up* "*Who's Who*".)

JANE. Mummy, I'll have a nervous breakdown if you don't sit still.

SHEILA (*returning with* "*Who's Who*" *above sofa*). It's all for you, my darling. Take your feet off. (JANE *takes feet off.*)

JANE. Thanks for nothing.

SHEILA. Nonsense, he's a very nice young man.

JANE. I hate young men.

SHEILA. Darling, I really do begin to think there's something wrong with you.

JANE. I know there's something wrong with him. He paws.

(SHEILA *begins to dial, having put* "*Who's Who*" *on table in front of sofa.*)

SHEILA. Oh, so you disapprove of that?

JANE. Well, really, Mummy, what a question.

SHEILA. Oh, I am so glad. I was afraid that you might look on pawing as a sort of early form of native dancing.

JANE. Not his sort of pawing, Mummy.

SHEILA (*at telephone*). Hello, Miss Grey? Good morning. (JANE *rises, crosses* U.S. *of sofa to breakfast table. Puts core in saucer. Sits* U.S. *chair.*) Has my husband . . . oh, he has. Yes, please. Oh, Jimmy, we've got David Bulloch dining now. So make it four. And Jimmy—don't ring off. I can't remember who his mother was. His father is Lord Cirencester, so Jane says. Rose Fripp? But Rosie died before the war. What do you mean, "that's right"? I've just been giving her my love. In what? A seance?—Oh, Jimmy, this is serious. He's gone. (*She seizes* "*Who's Who*".) It couldn't have been Rosie Fripp. He said that she was in the country.

JANE. P'raps she's buried there.

SHEILA. I sent her my love.

JANE. Well, there's no harm in that.

SHEILA. I've got it. Cirencester, John David Wilberforce, born 1911, married 1931 Rose Fripp, died 1937. It's true, Jane, it's too, too terrible. He must have thought me mad. I'll have to ring him up again. (*She seizes the telephone as it rings. At telephone.*) Hullo! Who do you want? Miss Broadbent? Oh yes, who is speaking? I'm her mother. David Bulloch? Yes, I'll tell her. Jane, it's David Bulloch.

> (JANE *gets her hand on the telephone as* SHEILA *snatches it back again.*)

What—David Bulloch! (*At telephone.*) Oh, David, this is Jane's mother again. (JANE *sits* U.S. *end of rostrum.*) I am so sorry to be such a bore. About your mother. I'm so sorry. Yes, I know she's dead. Yes, yes, I know it was. But I'm so sorry about asking you to give my love to her just now. (*To* JANE.) He says he can't because she's dead. (*At telephone.*) I know. That's why I'm so sorry. A long time ago! (*At telephone.*) Yes, David, it was a silly mistake to make. She couldn't help it. No, I made the mistake. When? Well, just now. You know I talked to you just now. But you must remember. (*To* JANE.) He says he hasn't spoken on the telephone—he must be goofy! You talk to him, Jane.

JANE (*at telephone*). Hullo! Yes. (*Sits on arm of sofa.*) Don't mind Mummy—she's all steamed up this morning. When? Tonight? But aren't you dining here? Oh. Hold on. I'll ask Mummy. (*To* SHEILA.) He wants me to dine with him tonight.

SHEILA. But darling child, he's dining here with us.

JANE. But he says he's not.

SHEILA. Has everyone gone mad? Jane, let me speak to him again.

JANE (*at telephone*). Hold on. Here's Ma. (*Rises behind sofa.*)

SHEILA (*at telephone*). David darling. This is Jane's mother. (JANE *sits on coffee table in front of sofa.*) I'm so sorry to be such a bore. I don't quite understand. I see. You wanted her to dine with you for Rhoda Gregson's dance. But, darling boy, you said that you'd dine with us. When? Five minutes ago. Excuse me, but you did. I talked to you for hours. That's when I spoke to you about your mother. David, I must know if I spoke on the telephone or not. I got your number from Mabel Crosswaite. (*To* JANE.) What number was it, Jane?

JANE. Oh, Mummy—Mayfair 6384.

SHEILA (*at telephone*). Mayfair 6384. That's not yours! Are you sure, David? My dear boy, do check up on the dial. You're at Caterham? (*To* JANE.) My dear, there's been some terrible mistake. (*At telephone.*) Oh, never mind the Sergeant Major. David, are you there? Hullo!

Are you quite sure you're David Bulloch? He's rung off ! (*She replaces the telephone.*)

JANE. No wonder. He must think you're crackers!

SHEILA. What is Mabel's number?

JANE. Sloane 7381.

SHEILA. What can have happened, Jane?

JANE. I wouldn't know.

SHEILA (*dialling*). If David Bulloch isn't dining here, who is?

JANE. I wouldn't know. You know, you ought to see a psycho-analyst. You really ought. You go round sending love to corpses on the telephone. You're half-way round the bend.

SHEILA (*replacing phone*). Engaged!

(*The telephone rings.*)

(*At telephone.*) Oh, Jimmy. Yes—Quaglino's. No—no, David Bulloch isn't coming now. There's been a terrible mistake. No, no! We'll still be four. I don't know, Jimmy. I don't know, I tell you. No, I'm perfectly all right. Please ring off, Jimmy. I must use the telephone. (*She replaces it, then picks it up.*) Sloane 73—

JANE. —81.

(SHEILA *dials.*)

(*Rises and takes a sweet from box on shelf.*) You ought to try that place at Tring if they'll have you, Mummy. Otherwise you'll find your-self inside a padded cell.

SHEILA (*at telephone*). Hullo! Oh, Mabel, this is Sheila. Your line's been engaged. Oh, has he? How nice! (*To* JANE.) David Bulloch's asked Clarissa out tonight. (*At telephone.*) But yes, darling, of course. Do bring him round for drinks. Oh, Mabel, by the way, I mustn't be a bore, but are you sure the number that you gave me did belong to David Bulloch? Not a bit. It doesn't matter. Still, just for fun, do ask Clarissa whose it was. (*To* JANE.) She's asking her. (*At telephone.*) *Whose?* David Hoylake-Johnston's? Really, how funny! Yes, wouldn't it have been? Good-bye! (*The forced laugh dies on her lips as she hangs up.*) What's the number, Jane?

JANE. The one Mabel gave us?

SHEILA. Yes, of course—

JANE. Mayfair 6384, Mummy.

SHEILA (*dialling*). I'll have to put him off.

JANE. Mummy, it's awfully rude.

SHEILA. I can't help that. He's—he's—he's not reliable. (*Listening into telephone.*) There's no reply.

JANE (*behind sofa*). Oh good.

SHEILA. I'll have to send a telegram.

JANE. But what's the matter with him, Mummy?

SHEILA (*re-dialling*). Everything. Aunt Mabel's told me all about him!

JANE. What?

SHEILA. I couldn't tell you, possibly . . .

JANE. Oh, Mummy!

SHEILA (*at telephone*). Hullo—is that telegrams? I'm Sloane 8479. (JANE *crosses to records on stool below radiogram.*) To David Hoylake-Johnston—I don't know—but does it matter? Well, then, put a "t" in if it makes you happy. No, I'm not being sarcastic. I'm extremely worried. No—no—not about the spelling. (*To* JANE.) What's the number, Jane?

JANE (*deliberately*). Mayfair 6284.

SHEILA (*at telephone*). Mayfair 6284. Regret must cancel invitation for tonight. Signed, Sheila Broadbent. With a "t". What? I've just told you. Oh, my own? Oh, how I wish I could remember numbers. (*She looks on the dial.*)

JANE (*turns on gramophone*). Yes, it is a help.

SHEILA. Sloane 8479. Good-bye. (*She sinks back, exhausted.*) Oh Jane, my darling child, I nearly made a terrible mistake.

JANE (*comforting her with a nice twinkle*). It's all right, Mummy. (*Dancing out of door* U.L.C.) Everybody makes them sometimes— even me!

> JANE *goes out, happy.* SHEILA *sinks back exhausted.*

CURTAIN

SCENE 2

The same evening. It is well past cocktail time.

> SHEILA, *in a house-coat, is standing by the bedroom door looking off* R. *The sitting-room door is open.*

SHEILA (*shouts*). Jane, darling.

JANE (*off*). What!

SHEILA. Where are you?

JANE (*off*). In the bath.

SHEILA. Well, hurry darling. Mabel and the others will be here at any minute.

JANE (*off*). All right. Don't flap, Mummy.

SHEILA (*shouting*). Don't forget that David Bulloch's coming round with Mabel, darling.

JANE (*off*). How I wish I could.

SHEILA. Now, don't be silly, darling. And hurry up.

> (*The telephone rings and she picks up the receiver.*)

Hello, Mrs. Broadbent speaking. Who? Business . . . I see. He'll be a little late. Thank you very much . . . Oh, and would you ask him to ring me as soon as he's dummy. (*She slams down the receiver.*)

> (MRS. EDGAR *opens the door.*)

MRS. EDGAR. Lady and Miss Crosswaite, madam.

> (MABEL *and* CLARISSA *enter.*)

MABEL. Sheila, we're here. How are you, darling? (MABEL *and* SHEILA *kiss.*)

> (*She comes in, followed by* CLARISSA, *who isn't spotty any more.*)

Are we much too early?

SHEILA. No. (MABEL *crosses below sofa.*) Would you believe—Jimmy is still playing bridge at Black's. And how's Clarissa?

> (*She kisses* CLARISSA.)

CLARISSA. All right, thanks, Aunt Sheila.

SHEILA. What a pretty dress! Wherever did you get it?

MABEL. From a little woman down in Pont Street.

CLARISSA. Mummy, she's the most enormous woman that I've ever seen—

MABEL (*sitting down*). We've had a simply dreadful day. I'm quite exhausted.

SHEILA. What have you been doing? Tell me, I just long to hear—

MABEL. Well, hair this morning. Twelve till half-past one—

SHEILA (*sweetly, to* CLARISSA). And what did you do, darling?

CLARISSA (*crossing* U.S. *to table in window to put down evening bag*). Hair as well.

SHEILA (*politely disbelieving*). Oh, really. Well, go on. (*Crosses above sofa to* U.S. *end of coffee table. Offers* MABEL *cigarette from box.*)

MABEL. We didn't lunch till two. Where did we snatch it, darling, in the end? (*To* SHEILA.) We had to grab it where we could.

CLARISSA. The Ritz.

MABEL. Oh yes, that's right. And in the afternoon, Clarissa simply dragged me round that most exhausting exhibition.

SHEILA. What did you think of it?

MABEL (*takes cigarette*). Quite terrible—although I must admit it made the Private Viewers look comparatively nice—

CLARISSA. You didn't understand the pictures, Mummy.

(SHEILA *lights cigarette for* MABEL, *then sits* U.S.R. *chair*.)

MABEL. Well, thank goodness for that. That sheep with seven eyes!

CLARISSA. That was symbolic.

MABEL. Yes, you've told me that before. (*To* SHEILA.) She keeps on saying that, but when I ask her what it was symbolic of, she doesn't know.

CLARISSA. I do!

MABEL. Well, tell me, darling.

CLARISSA. I've already told you.

SHEILA. Well, tell me. I'm simply dying to be told.

CLARISSA (*crossing to* SHEILA *below sofa*). It represents the beast in love.

SHEILA. My dear, how thrilling!

CLARISSA. And the green is envy. And the seven eyes are meant to be the seven deadly sins. And they're where they are because . . .

SHEILA. Where are they, darling?

MABEL. Anywhere but in the head, my dear!

SHEILA. It sounds enchanting. I can't wait to see it. Oh, I thought you were bringing David Bulloch with you.

MABEL. So we did. He's parking somewhere.

SHEILA. Oh, I see. (*To* CLARISSA.) You and your Davids! I was very nearly angry with you after breakfast.

MABEL. Nothing to what I was.

CLARISSA. Mummy, when? You weren't angry. You were . . .

MABEL. Darling, why not run along and talk to Jane?

SHEILA. Yes, what a good idea! You'll find her in her room. It's just beyond the bathroom on the left. Tell her to hurry up, from me! (*Rising and pushing* CLARISSA *out of door* U.L.C.)

(CLARISSA *goes.* SHEILA *crosses to drinks cupboard and gets out a bottle of gin. Takes it to drinks table in the window.*)

MABEL. Really, that child—she must be quite half-witted, making such a terrible mistake. I couldn't be more sorry, Sheila, but I never dreamed the horrid little creature had that dreadful bounder's number.

SHEILA. How did she get hold of it?

MABEL. My dear, she says she asked him for it last night at the dance.

SHEILA. How very forward of her.

MABEL. That's exactly what I said. And she said that it wasn't any worse than asking for an autograph. What happened, Sheila? Did you ring him up?

SHEILA. Of course I did, my dear. Well, actually I thought that he was David Bulloch, and I asked him if he'd dine tonight.

MABEL. My dear, did he accept?

SHEILA. Yes, like a shot. (*Back to drinks cupboard for glass.*)

MABEL. Of course he did. He's hardly had a single invitation since poor Brenda Barrington. He only went last night because old Mary Bickersteth's his aunt by marriage. Darling—but it's too exciting. When's he coming?

SHEILA (*back to drinks table*). He's not coming, thank the Lord. The moment I found out from you I put him off.

MABEL. You rang him up again? My dear, how too embarrassing.

SHEILA. I tried to, but he was out. I sent a telegram.

MABEL. My dear, how lucky that you rang me back. (*Rises and takes off coat, puts it on U.S.R. chair.*)

SHEILA. Well, David Bulloch luckily got on to Jane.

MABEL. Oh, did he, why?

SHEILA. He wanted her to dine with him.

MABEL (*coldly*). Oh, really.

SHEILA (*affecting not to notice this*). So of course it wasn't him that I'd been talking to.

MABEL. Poor Jane! What an escape she's had.

SHEILA. Tell me about him, Mabel. (*Crosses C.*) Have you got a hanky, darling? (*To dry her hands which have got wet on the shaker.*) He sounds simply fascinating.

MABEL. Well, his mother's an Italian.

SHEILA (*back to drinks table*). My dear, that's always dangerous.

MABEL. But don't I know it! Everybody seems to think that being married to a foreigner's a sort of compromise between a mistress and a wife, when in reality it couldn't be more homely usually I must admit, because the mistress angle's being taken care of on the side. At least, that's how Clarissa's father managed till I caught him out, and he was Scotch. Where was I, Sheila?

SHEILA. I don't know.

MABEL. Oh yes. David Hoylake-Johnston's mother. She was a Portofino, or a Positano— (SHEILA *to edge of rostrum.*) I forget—

but you know how they call themselves a lot of things if they're anything at all out there. My dear, it must have been a come-down to be just plain Mrs. Hoylake-Johnston after having lots of seaside holiday resorts strung through one's name like beads. But still she married him—he was a Consul in Milan, or something of that sort —and they had a son. Ah well, we've got to face it, Sheila, he's a menace. (*Crosses below sofa.*) Not one single debutante is safe. Not one. Well, look at Brenda Barrington. (*They both sit on sofa.*) My dear, I never told you all the story, did I? Well then, Nellie— you know, Nellie Barrington, she had a cocktail party for poor Brenda when the Season started, just before you came to London— and of all the people in the world, her husband brought him back.

SHEILA. Brought who back?

MABEL. The menace—the son. He praised up Brenda's dog, so Nellie said—a hideous old mongrel with bad breath and filthy habits. And then, at Cissy Orville's party that night at the River Room, he danced a waltz with Brenda, my dear, cheek-to-cheek, right from the start. Well, naturally, Nellie watched them like a hawk, right through the waltz, and then a foxtrot—then a sort of boogie-woogie thing with madly irritating music. Then she simply had to go off to the Ladies for a minute—

SHEILA. Brenda, dear, or Nellie?

MABEL. Nellie, darling—leaving Colonel Barrington on guard. When she came back he'd gone off to the bar, and they'd gone as well. And just as she was going to rush downstairs and try to catch them, well, of course, they *had* to play "The Queen"—and Nellie couldn't move. She stood there, simply rooted to the spot. My dear, she told me at the Derby that she never would have thought it possible that any piece of music could have lasted quite so long. And the most maddening thing of all, she said, was Colonel Barrington, who stood there like a poker with a sanctimonious expression on his face—when any sentry in his regiment who'd done what he'd done would have been court-martialled on the spot.

SHEILA. What happened?

MABEL. Well . . .

SHEILA. Oh . . . where?

MABEL. They never found that out. But does it matter? Probably his flat. He lives in bachelor chambers, as they call them, which is always a temptation in itself. But everyone knows what happened the weekend he stayed down with the Barringtons.

SHEILA. I don't. What did?

MABEL. My dear, Colonel Barrington found Brenda in flagrante de
. . . de . . . oh well.

(Phone starts ringing.)

You know what I mean: in David Hoylake-Johnston's room at
half past one at night.

SHEILA *(at telephone)*. You really are too naughty, Jimmy! Mabel and
Clarissa are both here, and simply furious. I don't care how much
they're over-playing, darling. Darling, it may be money for jam,
but why not tell your partner to stop. I've no patience with those
silly old men in Black's. Well, silly young men, then. (MABEL
crosses to drinks table with bag and leaves it on D.S. chair.) Six hearts.
He'd better get it. And you can tell him from me that I think he's
very selfish. What do you mean—I can tell him myself? When?
Tonight? At dinner? What are you talking about, Jimmy? Who
are you playing bridge with? David Hoylake-Johnston! Jimmy,
you're not to bring—! He's hung up! (*She replaces the telephone.*)
He can't have got my telegram. He's coming, Mabel.

MABEL. So I gathered, darling.

SHEILA. I must ring again and say he's got to stop him. (*She starts
dialling feverishly.*) What can I say, Mabel?

MABEL *(up to SHEILA)*. Really, it's a repetition of what happened at
the Barringtons'. I told you—didn't I?—how Colonel Barrington
brought him back to poor dear Nellie's flat.

SHEILA. Yes, yes, you did.

MABEL *(crossing D.L. on rostrum)*. I just can't wait to see what happens
when he gets here.

SHEILA. He won't get here if I have anything to do with it.

MABEL. I wonder if he'll talk to Jane about her dog?

SHEILA *(at telephone)*. Hullo—Black's? I want to speak to Mr. Broadbent. Yes, it is. Mabel, what can I say?

MABEL. Say Jane's got distemper.

SHEILA. Stop it, Mabel. (*At telephone.*) Yes? Oh dear. (*To MABEL.*)
He's left. (*At telephone.*) Was he alone? Another gentleman. I see.
Good-bye! (*She hangs up.*) He's coming, Mabel.

MABEL. With another gentleman!

SHEILA. Oh Mabel, I'll hit you.

MABEL. Sorry, darling.

SHEILA. Mabel, what am I to do?

MABEL. If I were you, I'd have a drink.

SHEILA (*going over to the drink table*). They mustn't be alone one single second. Not one single second!

MABEL. I'd like one too, if you don't mind.

SHEILA. It's just like Jimmy, making friends with such an awful man! He hasn't got an ounce of judgment. Not a solitary ounce!

MABEL (*crosses R. below sofa and turns*). Darling, be fair. He's only playing bridge with him. He didn't ask him out to dinner. I imagine David Hoylake-Johnston's very good at bridge—he sounds the type who knows exactly what he wants to make.

SHEILA. A cherry, Mabel?

MABEL. Thank you, darling.

(MRS. EDGAR *enters* U.L.C.)

MRS. EDGAR. Mr. Bulloch, madam.

MABEL. David, there you are. You know each other, don't you?

BULLOCH. No.

MABEL. Oh no, of course, you only knew his mother.

SHEILA. How do you do, David? I do hope you found somewhere nice to park.

BULLOCH. Yes, miles away, though. Almost back outside your flat, Lady Crosswaite.

(MABEL *crosses to* BULLOCH, *passes him and takes glass from* SHEILA. *Looks at records on stool and then places them on radiogram.*)

MABEL. Oh dear, poor you! Perhaps we should have come in a taxi.

BULLOCH. I thought of that. But if we had we would have had to take one back again to get the car.

SHEILA. Really, how fascinating! Would you like a cocktail?

BULLOCH. I'd love one. Thanks.

SHEILA. A cherry?

BULLOCH. I'd love one.

(MABEL *sits on stool.*)

SHEILA. Well then, there you are. (*Gives him hers.*)

BULLOCH. Oh, lovely, thanks! (*Pause.*) Are you going to Wimbledon this year?

SHEILA. No, I don't think so.

MABEL. Are you, David?

BULLOCH. No. (*Pause. Crosses below sofa.*) I went last year, though.

MABEL. So did I.

BULLOCH. I turned right over Chelsea Bridge. It took me straight there on the Brighton Road. Perhaps you went that way?

MABEL. I don't think so. We went by train.

(Pause.)

SHEILA *(to L. of sofa with drink).* I am so sorry about all that nonsense on the telephone this morning.

BULLOCH. Not a bit!

SHEILA. I do hope that the sergeant-major wasn't too annoyed.

BULLOCH. No, he was all right, really.

SHEILA. Well, he must have been. He gave you time to telephone Clarissa.

BULLOCH. Yes, rather. *(He looks nervously at MABEL.)*

MABEL. It's too sweet of you to take Clarissa out tonight!

BULLOCH. Oh, not a bit.

MABEL. Who are you dining with?

BULLOCH. Well, no one, actually.

MABEL. I thought Clarissa said it was a party.

BULLOCH. Oh, we're going on to Rhoda Gregson's dance, but we're not dining anywhere. I mean, not in a party.

MABEL. *Tête à tête.* I wonder if I ought to let you? What do you think, Sheila?

SHEILA. I'm quite sure you'll let them, darling.

(Enter CLARISSA U.L.C.)

CLARISSA *(to edge of rostrum).* Jane's not nearly ready yet. Oh, hullo, David!

BULLOCH. Hullo.

SHEILA. Well, I think I'll go and finish dressing. You see you entertain yourselves. Now, Mabel, will you see to the drinks?

MABEL. But I'll come with you, darling.

SHEILA. Oh, don't bother.

MABEL. It's no bother. *(Going out U.L.C. with a self-satisfied smile and toasting CLARISSA behind BULLOCH's back, closing door behind her.)*

(After MABEL and SHEILA have gone, there is a pause of some duration, during which BULLOCH is shy about CLARISSA's adoring gaze.)

BULLOCH. You doing Goodwood this year?

CLARISSA. Yes, I think so.

BULLOCH. Going down from London?

CLARISSA. Yes, are you?

BULLOCH. No, I'll be with friends in Hampshire. Down near Petersfield. I don't suppose you know them.

CLARISSA. Don't I?

R.D.—C

BULLOCH. Shouldn't think so. They're called Swayne.

CLARISSA (*crossing towards him behind sofa*). S-w-a-i-?

BULLOCH. No. Y.

CLARISSA. I don't think I know anyone called Swayne.

BULLOCH (*crosses* L. *below sofa*). Oh, then you wouldn't know them.

CLARISSA. No.

BULLOCH. It's quite a good idea to go by Harting.

CLARISSA. Is it?

BULLOCH. Yes, it saves the main road traffic on the Midhurst Road. You come in from the west, past a big place, called . . . I can't remember what it's called.

CLARISSA (R. *side of sofa*). It doesn't matter, David.

BULLOCH. But if you come down from London, you'll be coming from the north.

CLARISSA. Yes, I suppose I will.

BULLOCH. So Harting wouldn't be much use to you.

CLARISSA. No, I suppose it wouldn't.

　　　(*Long pause.* BULLOCH *moves behind chair* D.L.C.)

BULLOCH. Still, it might be useful one day if you find yourself in Hampshire during Goodwood Week.

CLARISSA. Yes, thanks.

BULLOCH. Oh, not a bit!

　　　(*Another interminable pause, during which* CLARISSA *fixes him again.*)

CLARISSA (*sits on sofa*). David, are you in love with Jane?

BULLOCH. Who? Me?

CLARISSA. Yes.

BULLOCH. I dunno.

CLARISSA. I do. You are. It happened last night at the dance.

BULLOCH. Oh, did it?

CLARISSA. Yes, I felt it.

BULLOCH. You did?

CLARISSA. Yes, you sort of went away from me.

BULLOCH. Oh, did I? Sorry!

CLARISSA. That's all right. Do your knees knock together when you see her?

BULLOCH (*towards her*). Yes, they do a bit.

CLARISSA. And does your tongue get dry?

BULLOCH. Yes, it does rather.

CLARISSA. Well, that's it.

BULLOCH. How do you know?

CLARISSA. That doesn't matter at the moment. David, it's no good, you know.

BULLOCH. How do you know?

CLARISSA. It's obvious. She just can't stand the sight of you. It's sticking out a mile. Why don't you give it up?

BULLOCH. Why should I?

CLARISSA. Well, for one thing it's so boring for your friends. Like going round with someone who's forgotten something.

BULLOCH (*moves away from her*). Sorry.

CLARISSA. I don't mind.

BULLOCH. Oh, don't you?

CLARISSA. No. It's your affair. Not mine. If you're going to go all broody, why should it hurt me?

BULLOCH (*sits in chair* D.L.C.). I don't know really. I just thought it did.

CLARISSA. You mean you think that I'm in love with you?

BULLOCH. Well, I did rather—actually.

CLARISSA. Oh, did you? Well, I'm not.

BULLOCH. Oh, sorry. (*Pause.*) I know what the place was called. The big place after Harting. It's West Dean.

CLARISSA (*almost in tears*). Oh, thanks.

(*Enter* JANE U.L.C., *in her evening dress.*)

JANE (*coldly*). Oh, hullo, David. (*Crosses below sofa to mirror.*)

BULLOCH (*rising*). Hullo, Jane.

JANE. Where's Mummy?

CLARISSA. Dressing.

(*Enter* MABEL U.L.C.)

MABEL (*going to* D.S. *end of sofa*). Darling Jane, how simply sweet you look! (BULLOCH *crosses to radiogram and looks at records.*) Who is it you remind me of? I know! Did you go to the Old Vic last winter? Well, I'll tell you. You look just like Juliet the evening she met what's his name.

(SHEILA *enters* U.L.C. *and turns on lights, then moves over to the tray and shakes the shaker violently.*)

SHEILA. Another cocktail, Mabel!

MABEL. Thank you, darling. (*She turns back to* JANE.) Every time I see that play I want to cry, don't I Clarissa?

CLARISSA. How should I know, Mummy?

MABEL. Darling child, of course I cry. (*Sitting.*) It wrings my heart to see that girl, so young and innocent and fresh to start with—

SHEILA. Mabel—

MABEL. —only to be utterly destroyed by love. Yes, darling?

SHEILA. Cherry? (*Crosses to sofa with drink.*)

MABEL. Thank you, darling. Good luck, darling.

SHEILA. Now, Clarissa, what will you have?

CLARISSA. Could I have a cocktail, please?

SHEILA. Of course. (*She returns to the tray.*)

JANE (*crossing to* U.L.). Oh, can I have one, Mummy?

SHEILA. No.

JANE. Why not?

SHEILA. Because I say not.

JANE. Mummy, honestly—

SHEILA. Be quiet! I've more important things to think about. That young man evidently didn't get my telegram.

JANE. Oh, didn't he?

SHEILA. No. There you are, Clarissa. (*She hands her a cocktail, crossing above sofa.*)

JANE. Does that mean he's coming?

SHEILA (D.R. *in front of kitchen door*). Yes. Your father's just been playing bridge with him in Black's.

JANE. So Daddy knows him?

SHEILA. Evidently.

JANE. Then he must be nice.

SHEILA. He isn't nice—so get that in your head.

JANE. But Daddy's friends are always nice.

SHEILA. They may be nice to Daddy, darling, but that doesn't mean that they're always nice to everybody else. He's a—he's—Mabel, what's the word I want?

MABEL. Well really, darling, are you sure you want it?

SHEILA. I know! A philanderer.

CLARISSA. I thought that that was someone who collected stamps.

SHEILA. What's Rhoda Gregson going to say?

JANE. She told us to bring anyone we liked.

SHEILA. But, darling, we don't like him. No one does.

MABEL. Except poor Brenda Barrington.

JANE. Mummy, he's not the man who—?

SHEILA. Jane, be quiet.

JANE. I say!

SHEILA (*to* MABEL). If we were in a party, like you were last night, it wouldn't be so bad.

MABEL. But you aren't, darling, are you?

SHEILA (*seeing* DAVID *looking at drinks*). Oh, David, would you like another drink?

BULLOCH. I'd love one.

SHEILA. Cocktail? (*Crossing to drinks.*)

BULLOCH. Yes, I'd love one.

SHEILA. Good. (*Works on it for him.*)

MABEL. Where are you two dining, David?

BULLOCH (*crossing to* MABEL). Oh, Quag's actually.

SHEILA. We're going there—

BULLOCH. Oh, good!

SHEILA. I've had a simply wonderful idea. (*Crosses to* BULLOCH *with his drink.*) Why don't we all join up and dine together?

BULLOCH. What, with me?

JANE (*crossing* D.S.L. *of* SHEILA). I'm sure that David doesn't want to, Mummy.

SHEILA. Oh, Jane darling, don't be silly. Of course he does. With Jimmy. It'll be such fun. Now say you will.

BULLOCH. I'd love to.

SHEILA (*triumphant*). Well, that's settled then. (BULLOCH *crosses* R. *to* U.S. *chair.*) I'll get on to them now and say we'll be—how many —one, two, three, four, seven—you'll come, Mabel, won't you?

MABEL. No really, darling.

SHEILA. Nonsense, darling, but of course you will. I simply won't allow you to go home and read the *Evening Standard* over a welsh rarebit. Now Jane, what's Quaglino's number?

JANE. How should I know, Mummy?

SHEILA. Never mind. I'm sure it's somewhere under "Q".

(*She goes to the telephone book and picks it up. There is a pause.*)

BULLOCH (*to* JANE). Are you going to Ascot this year, Jane?

(SHEILA *starts dialling.*)

JANE (*sitting chair* D.L.C.). No.

CLARISSA. I am.

BULLOCH. Yes, so am I. From London?

CLARISSA. No, from Staines. We're staying there. Do you know Staines at all?

BULLOCH. Yes, rather. It's a bottleneck.

(*During the first lines of the following dialogue,* SHEILA *signs to* BULLOCH *to hand round some food, which he does.*)

SHEILA (*at telephone*). Hullo! Is that Quaglino's? Oh, good evening!

This is Mrs. Broadbent speaking. Mrs. Jimmy Broadbent. I've a table in my husband's name for eight-thirty. That's right—for four. And Mr. David Bulloch has one booked for two—at—

BULLOCH. Eight-thirty.

SHEILA. Yes eight-thirty, too. Now could you put us all together at a table for—no, seven, yes, I know—but someone else is coming too. So even if we both agree that four and two makes six, another one makes seven. Thank you—now then, can you manage that? No, surely—not in some tiny corner? How much earlier? Yes, that'll be all right. Yes, yes, I promise. (*She rings off.*) That's all right, so long as we're there by eight.

JANE. It's ten to now.

SHEILA. Well, that's all right. I and your father will just have to follow on in a taxi. I'm so glad that it's all worked out all right. What fun it's going to be! (*Moves towards drinks table.*)

(SHEILA *smiles at* MABEL, *who does not return it. The door opens, and* JIMMY's *voice is heard.*)

JIMMY (*off*). You go right on in, old boy, and face the music. I'll run along and change.

(DAVID HOYLAKE-JOHNSTON *comes in* U.L.C.)

SHEILA. Good evening, Mr. Hoylake-Johnston! It's so nice of you to come. I'm Jimmy's wife. How do you do? Now let me introduce you—Mabel Crosswaite.

DAVID. How do you do? (*They shake hands.*)

SHEILA. And Clarissa—Mabel's girl. You know each other, don't you?

DAVID. Yes, we met last night.

SHEILA. And this is Jane, my daughter.

DAVID. How do you do?

(*As he puts out his hand to* JANE, SHEILA *catches it and takes him on to* BULLOCH.)

SHEILA. And then, David Bulloch.

DAVID ⎫ (*together*). ⎧Hullo, David.
BULLOCH ⎭   ⎨Hullo, David.

SHEILA. So you know each other?

DAVID. Yes, we met one weekend, staying in the country.

BULLOCH. At the Barringtons, actually.

SHEILA. Oh really, with the Barringtons! (*Crossing to drinks table below sofa.*) Now, Mr. Hoylake-Johnston, I'm quite sure you'd like a drink.

DAVID (*following* SHEILA *to above sofa*). Please call me David.

SHEILA. But I hardly know you!

DAVID. You've already made me feel at home.

SHEILA. Oh, really? Did you win your bridge?

DAVID. Oh yes, indeed.

MABEL. I'm sure you're very good.

DAVID. Oh no, your husband is the expert.

SHEILA. Have you known him long?

DAVID. No. I was standing by the bar, and Jimmy came and asked me to make up a four.

SHEILA. What a coincidence!

DAVID. Yes, wasn't it? Just like you on the telephone this morning.

MABEL. I declare it must be fate!

(SHEILA *goes over to get another drink.* DAVID *looks round, and decides to talk to* JANE.)

DAVID. Well, have you had a busy day?

JANE. Not very, I'm afraid.

DAVID. How very honest. Usually the answer is, "My dear, I'm utterly exhausted. Hair till lunch—and feet till two".

(CLARISSA *laughs.* DAVID *smiles charmingly at* MABEL, *who again does not return it.*)

Now let me guess exactly what you did. You took your dog in the park!

(SHEILA *jiggles with the shaker.*)

JANE. I haven't got a dog. At least I haven't got one here. I've got lots in the country, though. Do you like dogs?

DAVID. I'm sure I shall like all of yours.

JANE. My spaniel's just had puppies.

DAVID. Really? How exciting.

JANE. They're half fox-terrier. She met him in the village. I was in the chemist's, buying toothpaste.

SHEILA (*giving* DAVID *the drink*). Darling! (*She gets between* DAVID *and* JANE, *pushing him up on the rostrum.*) Oh, I beg your pardon. I'm quite sure Mr. Hoylake-Johnston doesn't want to hear about your dogs.

DAVID. Oh, but I do!

SHEILA. It's very nice of you to say so, but I'm sure you don't. After your time out in Malaya, I'm afraid we must seem too parochial for words.

DAVID. What nonsense!

SHEILA. Do you know, I'm really quite ashamed of asking you to come tonight to go to a deb dance with these young people.

(SHEILA *gesticulates with the hand containing the cocktail shaker, nearly knocking* JANE's *head.* BULLOCH *misunderstands her.*)

BULLOCH. Yes, I'd love a drop more. (*Rises and crosses to* SHEILA *with glass.*)

DAVID. But I'm looking forward to it quite tremendously.

JANE. Do you like dancing?

DAVID. Yes, I love it.

MABEL. I expect you're very good at it.

DAVID. Well, actually, I had some lessons when I was in Singapore. I made a habit of it when I came back from the jungle. I got mad about it after watching native dances in the little villages.

SHEILA. Oh really! But how interesting.

JANE. What sort of dancing do they do out there?

DAVID. Oh, very primitive, but beautiful. The loveliest of all's a sort of wedding dance. You know, when a chief's daughter's getting married. It goes on for hours and hours. The whole tribe joins in first of all until they get exhausted. Then the numbers gradually get less and less, until the bride and bridegroom are left dancing on their own. It's wonderful to watch them, with the moonlight shining through the rubber-trees, their bodies swaying to the rhythm, and the movements getting more and more interpretive.

(SHEILA's *hand involuntarily clutches* MABEL.)

And then the music rising to a climax and then suddenly it sort of shudders into silence and he picks her up and kisses her and carries her away to his tent.

JANE. Go on.

SHEILA. But Mr. Hoylake-Johnston's finished, darling. Jane, Jane. Run and get your coat, Jane; go and get your coat. (*Exit* JANE. *To* DAVID.) I'm sorry we're rushing off the moment you've got here, but we're all dining together at Quaglino's, and they said they couldn't fit us in much after eight. Now cars: who's got a car?

DAVID. I have.

BULLOCH. I have. Mine's only a two-seater, I'm afraid.

DAVID. So's mine. And open.

SHEILA. Oh.

MABEL (*rising below coffee table to coat in* U.S.R. *chair*). I'm sure Jane would love that, Sheila. Open cars are so exhilarating—

SHEILA. I'm afraid I can't allow that, with her sinus.

MABEL. Has Jane got a sinus?

SHEILA. Yes, poor child. I know. If Mr. Hoylake-Johnston took Clarissa—

MABEL (*cutting in*). Darling, if Jane's really got a sinus, she must go to Clarissa's doctor. He's too marvellous. He says if she keeps out of draughts she may not need the operation.

SHEILA. Really, but you've never mentioned it before.

MABEL. Darling, I simply can't abide health talk . . . (*She smiles at* DAVID.) being so rudely fit myself.

SHEILA. Well, as you're so healthy, we'll send you in the open car. How's that?

DAVID. Delighted.

MABEL. Thank you so much, darling. (*She is beaten, but she has one more shot. To* CLARISSA.) Well, Clarissa, you'll go with David then?

CLARISSA. Yes, Mummy.

SHEILA. That's right. And I'm sure that you can squeeze in Jane as well.

BULLOCH (*delighted*). Yes, rather!

SHEILA (*smiling at the furious* MABEL). Then that's perfect. And then me and Jimmy'll come in a taxi. (*To* MABEL.) Hurry, darling, or we'll lose the table.

(BULLOCH *helps* MABEL *to put on coat.*)

MABEL. Now where's my bag?

DAVID. Is this it? (*Picking it up from chair.*)

MABEL. Yes. Good-bye, darling, look after yourself. (*Crosses to* L.C. *in doorway.*) Well, Sheila, if I get pneumonia, I'll sue you with both lungs.

(MABEL *and* DAVID *go.* JANE *comes in* U.L.C. *with her coat.*)

JANE. Where's he gone?

SHEILA. Only Quaglino's, darling.

JANE. With Aunt Mabel?

SHEILA. Yes, he's giving her a lift.

JANE. Why her?

SHEILA. Well, why not, darling? David's very kindly taking you two.

(JANE *looks furious and* CLARISSA *looks delighted.*)

(*To* BULLOCH.) Now then, David, are you ready with your load?

BULLOCH. Yes, rather!

CLARISSA (*rising*). Oh, dear!

SHEILA. What's the matter?

CLARISSA. I think I've split something! Jane, you haven't got a pin?

JANE. Yes, hundreds, in my room.

SHEILA. Oh, I'll come and help you.

>   (CLARISSA *goes out* U.L.C. *followed by* SHEILA.)

Jane, ring up for a taxi, darling, while you're waiting. I must go and hurry up your father. (*She goes out.*)

>   (JANE *goes to the telephone and starts dialling.* DAVID BULLOCH *seizes her.*)

JANE. David, go away. (*At telephone.*) Oh, could we have a taxi please at fourteen Victor Court? (*She hangs up.*)

BULLOCH. I love you, Jane!

>   (SHEILA *comes in* U.L.C.)

SHEILA. Where's my glass? (*Her face lights up as she sees the scene.*) Oh darlings—I'm so sorry! Never mind! (*She nips out again, down the passage.*)

BULLOCH. Jane, let me kiss you!

JANE. No.

BULLOCH. I must.

JANE. I won't!

>   (*He seizes her and she struggles violently back in a sinister silence.*
>
>   *During this,* JIMMY, *in his shirt sleeves, comes in* U.L.C., *goes across, pours out a cocktail, and starts back with it to his room without taking any notice of the scene.*
>
>   *As he is going,* JANE *slaps* DAVID BULLOCH's *face. The struggle stops, and* JANE *sees* JIMMY.)

Oh, this is David Bulloch, Daddy.

JIMMY. Oh, good evening! Hope you're getting all you want. (*He goes out, leaving them together.*)

CURTAIN

ACT TWO

SCENE I

The time is early morning. The flat is in darkness, but the passage light is on.

SHEILA *throws open the sitting-room door, and switches on the light, but before she does that she shouts in the passage.*

SHEILA. Jane, darling, are you in? (*Coming into the sitting-room.*) Jimmy, look in her room.
JIMMY (*off*). All right.
    (SHEILA *switches on the light and comes into the sitting-room with a worried look on her face. She goes to the kitchen door and opens it.*)
SHEILA. Jane! Jane!

             (JIMMY *comes in.*)

JIMMY. She's not in.
SHEILA. Jimmy, what are we to do?
JIMMY (*crossing towards the kitchen door*). What can we do? Wait and see.
SHEILA (*at fireplace*). Oh, Jimmy, you are useless!
JIMMY. Have a drink?
SHEILA. I wonder if we ought to?
JIMMY. Why the devil not?
SHEILA. Well—Jane—
JIMMY. It won't make any difference to Jane how much we drink. It's what she drinks that matters. (*Exit into kitchen, switching on light.*)
SHEILA (*moving D.C. round D.S. arm of sofa*). No! I hadn't thought of that. You don't think he'll make her drunk?
JIMMY (*off*). Depends how much he gives her.
SHEILA. Oh, how can you be so callous, Jimmy?
JIMMY (*off*). Well, you asked me, darling. (*Noise of champagne cork.*)
SHEILA. How much drink would make her—make her—
JIMMY (*off*). Make her drunk?
SHEILA. Well, yes.
JIMMY (*off*). Depends how strong her head is.

SHEILA. Oh, thank goodness it isn't bad. Do you remember when she had some cherry brandy at the Point-to-Point, and backed two winners afterwards?

JIMMY (*in kitchen doorway*). Oh, well, that's hopeful.

SHEILA. It's not funny, Jimmy.

JIMMY. No—I know it isn't. Here, hold that. (*Gives her a glass. As he pours:*) But still, it's no use letting your imagination run away with you. (*Having poured his own out.*) To absent friends. To Jane. Good luck to her!

SHEILA. To Jane . . . (*Sits on sofa.*) Oh . . . (*Bursts into tears.*)

JIMMY. Don't cry, darling. What's the matter now?

SHEILA. I feel so awful, Jimmy. And it's all my fault: I asked that dreadful bounder here, and if I hadn't, David Bulloch would have asked Jane out tonight. Oh, dear . . .

JIMMY. She's well out of that, if you ask me! I thought he looked, well, over half way round the bend.

SHEILA. His father's got a lovely place in Warwickshire.

JIMMY (*sits chair* U.S.R.). What Bulloch Hall? Who gave you all this gossip?

SHEILA. It's all in the Peerage.

JIMMY. I was going to say I didn't think you'd got it out of David Bulloch. Hardly heard him utter once tonight, except to tell some wretched girl the way to Pontefract. Is Mabel interested in David Bulloch for Clarissa?

SHEILA. Well, of course. Don't be silly. She was terrified at dinner he was getting interested in Jane.

JIMMY. Oh—was she?

SHEILA. Darling, don't men ever notice anything?

JIMMY. Yes, some things.

SHEILA. I think David Bulloch's very fond of Jane, in fact I'm sure he is. But how was I to know he was, when I invited David Hoylake-Johnston? He'd only seen her once. Oh dear—I've ruined Jane for life. What shall I do?

JIMMY (*rises, picks up champagne bottle from sofa table*). Fill up your glass, old girl. (*He fills both the glasses.*) If horses went to dances, they'd be in clover. They sleep standing up.

SHEILA. Am I supposed to laugh at that?

JIMMY (*turns on light*). It's optional, my dear. How old Harold Gregson ever married Rhoda beats me.

SHEILA. She owns half Yorkshire.

JIMMY (*crosses to drinks table for swizzle stick*). Even so I'd sooner settle for the other half. Harold was saying the grouse have got disease this year.

SHEILA. Poor things.

JIMMY. Comes from not shooting them, he says.

SHEILA. Well, obviously they won't get it if you shoot them.

JIMMY. No. It's due to overcrowding.

SHEILA. Oh!

JIMMY (*crosses to* SHEILA *and uses swizzle stick in her glass*). If Rhoda Gregson's friends were grouse, the death rate would be pretty high. I thought she looked a bit like Groucho Marx tonight, except that her moustache was darker. Which was the Gregson girl?

SHEILA. In green, fair-haired.

JIMMY. Not that pretty creature? Isn't nature wonderful? As far as I remember, she was totally clean shaven.

SHEILA. Well, she's only seventeen.

JIMMY. Well, let's hope that she takes after Harold.

SHEILA (*whose mind has not been on the conversation at all*). If Dickie and Louisa hadn't come and talked to me, I would have seen them go. They must have disappeared like that. Louisa said, "Sheila, I'm simply dying to see Jane. I hear she's too divine for words, and Dickie's mad to dance with her". And I said, "That's her with the dark young man"—and pointed at her and she wasn't there. She must have gone while I was talking to Louisa.

JIMMY (*round behind sofa to put down swizzle stick on shelf*). Yes, most careless of you, darling.

SHEILA. Me. What about you!

JIMMY. What about me? I watched that girl from half past ten to half past one, when you took over.

SHEILA. That's not very long.

JIMMY. Not very long! I'll have you know that sentries only do two hours. Like a cigarette?

SHEILA. Yes, please. (JIMMY *hands her a cigarette from box on shelf, also lighter from shelf.*) I'm sorry, Jimmy. What's the time?

JIMMY. Three.

SHEILA. Jimmy, how long does it take a native dancer to get hotted up?

JIMMY. I wouldn't know. Depends what time of day it is, I shouldn't wonder.

SHEILA. I don't mean that kind of hotting up.

JIMMY. No. I don't either. And on who he's dancing with. Why? Was it in a crossword?

SHEILA. No. I only wondered. Jimmy, do you think he's taken her back to his tent?

JIMMY. His what?

SHEILA. I mean his flat.

JIMMY. Quite possibly.

SHEILA. You don't!

JIMMY. It has been done.

SHEILA. Oh, Jimmy, we'll have to ring him up.

JIMMY. Why not?

SHEILA. What can we say?

JIMMY. Well, ask to speak to Jane.

SHEILA. Oh, what a good idea! (*Goes to telephone.*) What's the number?

JIMMY. I don't know.

SHEILA. I don't know either, Jimmy.

JIMMY. Who does know?

SHEILA. Jane wrote it on the table-cloth this morning.

JIMMY (*sitting on sofa*). Well, then—where's the table-cloth?

SHEILA (*moves slightly in direction of table*). It all depends what day it is.

JIMMY. It's Thursday now.

SHEILA. That means that it was Wednesday this morning.

JIMMY. It's this morning now.

SHEILA. Oh, don't be so confusing, Jimmy. All I want to know is, was it Wednesday when we had breakfast yesterday?

JIMMY. Yes, very probably.

SHEILA. Then it's gone.

JIMMY. What has?

SHEILA. The table-cloth! The laundry goes on Wednesday.

JIMMY. Bad luck.

SHEILA (*opens curtains, looks out, then closes curtains*). It must be fate. Oh, poor poor Jane!

JIMMY (*puts his feet up on the sofa*). Where did Jane get the number in the first place?

SHEILA. I got it.

JIMMY. Where from?

SHEILA. From Mabel.

JIMMY. Mabel!

SHEILA. Yes, she gave it to me by mistake for David Bulloch's.

JIMMY. Did she now?

SHEILA. I've got to have that number, Jimmy! Every minute counts!

JIMMY. Ring Mabel, then.

SHEILA. She won't be back.

JIMMY. She will. She never went.

SHEILA. Well, she'll be asleep.

JIMMY. The telephone'll wake her.

SHEILA. Poor, poor Mabel!

JIMMY. Which do you prefer, poor, poor Mabel or poor, poor Jane?

SHEILA (U.S. *towards telephone*). I daren't, Jimmy.

JIMMY. Why not?

SHEILA. She's the biggest gossip ever born.

JIMMY. We've got to risk it.

SHEILA. Risk it—it's a certainty.

JIMMY. Well, gossip's better than the other thing—

SHEILA. Jimmy! You can't think that of your own daughter.

JIMMY. Yours as well!

SHEILA. What do you mean by that?

JIMMY. Nothing. Have some more champagne. (*He refills her glass.*)

SHEILA. How selfish we are, Jimmy, drinking when Jane's—

JIMMY. Nonsense, it'll do you good!

SHEILA (*drinks. In doorway*). He is good-looking, isn't he?

JIMMY. Who?

SHEILA. David Hoylake-Johnston.

JIMMY. I suppose so, if you like that type of man.

SHEILA. Well, naturally I do. He's every woman's type. (*Coming back into the room.*) Tall, lean and handsome. Dark, broad-shouldered —what more could one want?

JIMMY. Nothing, I hope.

SHEILA. Don't, Jimmy!

JIMMY. Ring up Mabel. Go on! If you don't, I will!

SHEILA. Oh no, Jimmy, you mustn't. It'd sound much too important, if you did. I know—I'll ask her round for drinks tomorrow. (*Starts dialling.*)

JIMMY. What, at three a.m.?

SHEILA. No, seven.

JIMMY. Darling, it's three now. Hardly the moment to start sending invitations out.

SHEILA. Give me that glass . . . (JIMMY *gets* SHEILA's *glass from sofa table and hands it to her. She dials. Nothing happens.*)

JIMMY. Give it a chance. I'll bet she snores like hell!

SHEILA (*at telephone*). Oh, hullo, Mabel darling! This is Sheila. Sheila! Sheila Broadbent. Did I wake you? I'm so sorry. Very early, yes. I'm sorry to be such a bore—but could you give me David Hoylake-Johnston's number? Yes, I know you did. But I've mislaid it—it's gone to the wash. It doesn't matter, darling. But I haven't got it. No, it's only Jane left her bag in his car—and Jimmy's so afraid it may be stolen in the night. Thanks so much, darling! (*To* JIMMY.) Looking in Clarissa's book. (*To telephone.*) Mayfair 6384. You are an angel, darling! Isn't she? Oh, Jane's been in for hours! We brought her back quite early. She was very tired, poor darling. Well, good night, Mabel darling—sorry to have woken you. (*She hangs up.*) I knew it—she's suspicious!

JIMMY. How do you know?

SHEILA. She wasn't angry, and that means she was interested. Now what's the number?

JIMMY (*writing it down on the back of a book of matches*). 6384 Mayfair.

SHEILA (*dialling*). And Clarissa's not in yet. She must be out with David Bulloch. They're probably engaged by now. (*Coming* D.S. *with telephone.*) No answer.

JIMMY. Let it ring a bit—he's probably asleep.

SHEILA. Jimmy! (*She sits in chair* D.S.L. *and lets the phone ring.*) Oh, Jimmy, how are we to know if he's deliberately not answering?

JIMMY. We're not.

SHEILA (*holding it*). I can see him now, holding her away from the telephone—her strained, frightened little eyes, looking beseechingly up into his. His tense body waiting for the telephone to stop ringing.

JIMMY. Well—let it go on ringing.

SHEILA. Why—what difference will that make?

JIMMY. Well, anybody who's in the least bit sensitive—
                    (SHEILA *continues to hold it.*)

SHEILA. Oh, Jimmy, what are we to do?

JIMMY. I'm all for bed—

SHEILA. How can you?

JIMMY. Well, what else do you suggest we do?

SHEILA. We've got to find them. If we find them—we might save the day.

JIMMY. Like Blücher.

SHEILA. Blücher?

JIMMY. Blücher saved the day at Waterloo.

SHEILA. Well, there you are—

JIMMY. But I expect he had a map reference.

SHEILA (*replacing the receiver*). I'm going to put it back. She might be trying to ring us. Ought we to ring the police?

JIMMY. What for?

SHEILA. To tell them Jane's not in.

JIMMY. I doubt if they'd be interested.

SHEILA (*rising for glass, leaving telephone on the floor*). How can you be so heartless. Don't you see, we'll have to pack her off abroad, like Brenda Barrington.

JIMMY. You don't mind jumping to conclusions, do you?

SHEILA. Well, with that young bounder. (*To window.*) If only we knew where she was.

JIMMY. What does it matter where?

SHEILA. Who's jumping to conclusions now?

JIMMY. I'm damned if I'm not catching it from you.

SHEILA. Oh, Jimmy, I can't bear it!

JIMMY. What's the matter now?

SHEILA (*closing C. door. Gets wrap from sofa. Puts it on*). Poor darling Jane! If only we were back to April—just before we came to London—when she had no thought of anything but playing croquet with her Daddy—and then now—! (*Moves below sofa R.*)

JIMMY. You know, you women beat me altogether. Just look at you! You think of nothing but this blasted London season all the winter. You rehearse it at Hunt Balls and so on and so forth. Then, when you get to the opening night, so to speak, you can't take it.

SHEILA. I don't know what you're talking about!

JIMMY. Of course you do. It's all your own fault—you and all the other mothers like you, behaving like a lot of refined White Slave traffickers.

(SHEILA *goes over and squats near the fire.*)

You bring a perfectly sweet and charming girl up from the country —a girl that even the Vicar's daughters have been proud to call their friend—

SHEILA. Why bring them up?

JIMMY. Because they typify the decent life that Jane's led up to now.

SHEILA (*sits on floor in front of fire*). That's what you think. I'll have you know a lot of people say that Bella isn't all that she's cracked up to be since the Hunt Ball.

JIMMY. I daresay not. Her mother didn't plan it, though, like you did. It was just an accident. I mean to say—no one could possibly have known that that dreadful fellow in the hired red coat had got her in the potting shed. I mean to say her mother didn't put her there and then ring up the fellow—

SHEILA. Jimmy, don't!

JIMMY. I'm sorry, but we may as well face facts. In Bella's case it was an accident. And like all accidents, exciting and deplorable. But in our case it's different. Far less exciting and far more deplorable, because it's planned. We bring Jane up to London, throw her on the town with fifteen hundred pounds' worth of advertisement, dress her up in silks and satins, have her hair washed at five pounds a time, and then sit back and wait. And all for what? You don't have to tell me. I know well enough. To catch the eye of the young men. Can you deny that, Sheila? Can you possibly deny that that's the object of the exercise?

SHEILA. Well, naturally, we all want Jane to look her best.

JIMMY. With what object in view?

SHEILA. Well, don't you want your daughter looking nice?

JIMMY. Not if it leads to this.

SHEILA. This was an accident.

JIMMY. An accident indeed! We sit all through the summer waiting for a victim, like a fellow waiting for a tiger with a goat tied to a stake. When the tiger doesn't come, what do we do? Only ring up the biggest man-eater in London and invite him round to have a meal. Then, when he carries the goat off somewhere in the bush, you say it was an accident. The whole thing's fundamentally immoral!

SHEILA (*rising and crossing back in front of sofa towards door*). Have you finished?

JIMMY. No. You just can't take it, that's what's wrong with you. You're like a woman on a race-course. You put everything you've

got on some damned horse, and if it wins the sun comes out. But if
it loses, you're in the car park long before the jockeys have weighed
in. If you can't take it, then you shouldn't bet. In other words,
you shouldn't put your daughter in the Marriage Stakes, however
big the prizes are, in case she falls.

(*The telephone rings.*)

SHEILA (*at telephone*). Hullo, Jane darling. (*She checks suddenly.*) Oh,
Mabel. Yes, so silly of me. I forgot she was in for a moment. Oh,
how sweet of you to worry, darling. Yes. I did. And he promised
to look in his car although he was in bed. Too sweet of him.
What, darling? Oh, have they? Did they have a good time?
Zizzi's. Oh, how lovely. Good night, darling. I must stop or
Jimmy'll wake up. (*She hangs up.*) David Bulloch brought Clarissa
back and they told Mabel Jane and David Hoylake-Johnston were
at Zizzi's.

JIMMY. What on earth is Zizzi's?

SHEILA (U.S. *to telephone books*). Don't be silly, you remember, darling.
We took Jane there on her birthday.

JIMMY. Not that damned cellar—with those fellows blowing trumpets
down one's ear at point-blank range. Too primitive for words.

SHEILA (*gives phone book to* JIMMY). Don't, Jimmy, don't. Here. Look
the number up.

JIMMY. Well, anyway, a night-club's better than a flat.

SHEILA. Oh, how I hope so.

JIMMY. Well, of course it is. I mean to say, two sardines can't get up
to much inside their tin.

SHEILA (*sitting in chair* D.L., *ready to dial*). I lied to Mabel and she knew
that I was lying. She'll have it all round London in the morning.
It'll ruin Jane.

JIMMY. She can't talk.

SHEILA. Can't she?

JIMMY. She let David Bulloch take Clarissa.

SHEILA. That's quite different. He's a gentleman.

JIMMY. Oh, is he? Yes, I see. Here we are, Zizzi's. Gerrard 2446.

(SHEILA *goes over to dial.*)

It beats me how that place keeps open. I thought dancing to a tom-tom and a penny-whistle was confined to cannibals. Come to think of it, perhaps it still is.

SHEILA (*at telephone*). Hullo. Oh, is that Zizzi's? Oh, it is. And is that Mr. Zizzi speaking? You're Bert? I see, and who is Bert? Bert Brown? I see. Good evening, Mr. Brown. I was just wondering if I could speak to my daughter. How do you know she ain't? Oh, I see. I'm so sorry to have troubled you. Good night—er—good morning. (*She hangs up.*)

JIMMY. Had Bert passed out?

SHEILA. No. He was the night watchman. They're closed. Oh, Jimmy, what'll happen if she brings him back here for a drink?

JIMMY. I'm not a prophet, darling.

SHEILA. She'll see that we've been waiting up for her.

JIMMY. Well, so we have.

SHEILA (*rising, crossing* U.S. *behind sofa*). She mustn't, Jimmy. Psychologically it's wrong to let her see that we are worried. Even if she isn't interested in David Hoylake-Johnston, if we look as if we'd be against it if she was, she will be.

JIMMY (*repeating—bewildered*). If she was, she will be—

SHEILA. What I mean is that we've got to wait up—but she mustn't know we are— (*Tries to move* JIMMY *off the sofa.*)

JIMMY. What—up the chimney?

SHEILA. Don't be silly, Jimmy—in the kitchen. Then we'll hear if we're wanted.

JIMMY. But we won't be wanted. If it's all above board, then we won't be wanted. If it isn't, we won't be wanted either.

SHEILA. Yes, we will—if he assaults her. (*Runs to the door.*)

JIMMY. Where are you going now?

SHEILA. I was seeing if our door's shut. Now, you go into the kitchen.

JIMMY. Into the kitchen? (*Rising.*)

SHEILA. Darling—and see if you can hear me!

JIMMY. I can hear you from here.

SHEILA. Darling, do try and understand. We're hiding in the kitchen, and we've got to hear what's going on—so run along.

JIMMY. Yes, rather!

(JIMMY *goes into the kitchen, leaving* SHEILA *in the room.*)

SHEILA. Jimmy!

JIMMY (*coming back*). What's the matter?

SHEILA. Shut the door.

JIMMY. I thought that we'd hear better with it open.

SHEILA. Jimmy, shut that door!

JIMMY. Yes, right, my dear!

> (*He again goes into the kitchen and shuts the door, leaving* SHEILA *alone once more. She takes off evening wrap and puts it on chair* D.L.)

SHEILA (*turning away from kitchen door*). Don't! Don't! How dare you! Take your hands off me, you beast . . .

JIMMY (*rushing in*). What's the matter? What's the matter, darling?

SHEILA (*to* JIMMY). Did you hear me?

JIMMY. Yes, of course I did!

SHEILA. Well, that's all right—the moment that we hear her key, we'll turn the lights out here and nip in there—you understand?

JIMMY. Yes, darling—but what happens if she doesn't kick up a shindy?

SHEILA (*crossing towards him*). Don't be silly, but of course she would.

JIMMY. He might have gagged her with a handkerchief.

SHEILA. What, in the street?

JIMMY. No, here.

SHEILA. Well—we'd hear that all right.

JIMMY. I doubt it. Handkerchiefs don't make much noise.

SHEILA. Oh, Jimmy, he'd say things as he tied it on.

JIMMY. Perhaps, but only in an undertone.

SHEILA. How do you know?

JIMMY. Well, naturally his passions are aroused—

SHEILA. Then he'd make a noise.

JIMMY. No—not that kind of passion.

SHEILA. Well, you make some passion noises, and I'll see if I can hear you. (*She goes towards the kitchen and turns at the door.*) Isn't this tremendous fun! (*She nips happily into the kitchen and shuts the door.*)

JIMMY (*alone, shouting*). You ready, darling?

SHEILA (*coming back*). But I thought you said he wouldn't make a noise.

JIMMY. Go back. I haven't started yet.

> (SHEILA *goes back.*)

(*Alone again.*) Ha, ha! My pretty dove! I've got you now. Ha, ha!

SHEILA (*coming back*). What are you laughing at?

JIMMY (*furiously*). Go back! That's just the way they do it.

SHEILA. Sorry! (*She goes back again, shutting door.*)

JIMMY (*alone, playing his part with relish*). Ha! I love you! Don't you understand? You devil—you divinity . . . you *woman!* Can't you see I love your innocent and frightened eyes! I love—

(*Enter* JANE, U.L.C.)

JANE. Daddy, I think it's high time you were in bed. Where's Mummy?

JIMMY. In the kitchen.

(JANE *goes to the door* D.R., *opens it, and* SHEILA *falls into the room.*)

SHEILA. Jane! Hullo, darling! (*Moving* U.S.) We were just going to bed.

JANE. Oh, good.

SHEILA. Darling, where have you been?

JIMMY. To Rhoda Gregson's dance.

SHEILA. Be quiet, Jimmy. I'm asking Jane. Jane, darling? Where have you been?

JANE (*removes gloves and stole, puts them on chair below kitchen door*). Out with David, Mummy.

SHEILA. David Hoylake-Johnston?

JANE. Yes.

SHEILA. Where to?

JANE. Oh, almost everywhere.

JIMMY. Hang on to "almost", Sheila.

SHEILA. Jimmy, please be quiet. (*To* JANE.) What do you mean by "almost everywhere"?

JANE. Oh, I don't know, Mummy. You ask him, Mummy. He'll know.

SHEILA. How can I ask him if he isn't here?

JANE. He is. He's coming up. He's gone back for my bag—I left it in the car.

JIMMY. That's one in the eye for Mabel.

SHEILA. He'll wake up Mrs. Edgar.

JANE. No, he won't. He's got my key.

SHEILA. Why is he coming up?

JANE. Because I asked him to.

SHEILA. What for?

JANE. To have a drink.

SHEILA. A drink! Darling! At four o'clock?

JANE. Well, what else could I offer him?

JIMMY. Yes—what indeed?

SHEILA. Jimmy, why don't you go to bed?

JIMMY. Why don't we all? I mean, you and I.

(*Enter* DAVID HOYLAKE-JOHNSTON, U.L.C.)

DAVID. May I come in?

SHEILA (*all sweetness and light*). Good evening, Mr. Hoylake-Johnston. How sweet of you to bring Jane home! (*Crossing above sofa towards him.*)

DAVID. That was the least that I could do. (*To* JIMMY.) Hello!

JIMMY (*rising*). Hullo! Have you had fun?

DAVID. Yes, rather! I've been showing Jane the hot-spots.

SHEILA. Oh, how kind of you.

JANE. We danced and danced and danced.

SHEILA. Oh, really, darling. How exciting!

JANE. Yes, it was.

DAVID. I'm sorry that I didn't ask you if you minded Jane and me departing, but we couldn't see you anywhere.

SHEILA. Oh, that's all right! We quite forgot about you—didn't we, Jimmy?

JIMMY. Yes, we forgot all about you! I'm off to bed. Jane, you know where the drinks are.

JANE. Thank you, Daddy.

JIMMY. David'll know which is which. Come along, darling. I'd like a nap before the office, if you wouldn't mind.

(*Exit* JIMMY U.L.C.)

SHEILA. All right. Good night, then, Mr. Hoylake-Johnston.

DAVID. Good night—and thank you for a most delightful evening!

SHEILA. Not at all! (*Kissing* JANE.) Now darling, don't stay up too late. (*Exit* U.L.C.)

(JANE *goes and shuts the door, which* SHEILA *has left hopefully open.*)

DAVID. I hope your mother's not too angry with me—

JANE (*picking up telephone and glass from floor and putting them back* U.S.). Don't mind Mummy—have a drink?

DAVID. Yes, please.

JANE. What can I offer? Knowing Daddy, I should say there's everything but water!

DAVID. I'd love some water.

JANE. Would you really?

(DAVID *nods.*)

I'll have to get it from the kitchen. (*She goes halfway to the door and turns.*) Would you like a rich tea biscuit?

DAVID. Yes, I'd love one.

JANE. Oh, good. So would I!

(JANE *turns and opens the door into the kitchen and* SHEILA *comes through it again.*)

Mummy, what are you doing?

SHEILA. I was looking for my ear-rings, darling.

JANE. Which ones?

SHEILA. The diamonds.

JANE. But you weren't wearing them.

SHEILA. Oh, wasn't I? Then it must be the gold ones . . .

DAVID. Can I help you, Mrs. Broadbent?

SHEILA. No, no—please don't bother! I'm quite happy looking for them!

(JANE *has gone into the kitchen.* SHEILA *and* DAVID *look about the room.*)

DAVID (*finding the ear-rings behind ashtray, under drinks cupboard*). Gold, you said?

SHEILA. I think so.

DAVID. Would these be them?

SHEILA. No, I don't think so. But—yes! How too extraordinary! I must have left them there this . . . How too kind of you. I couldn't be more grateful.

JANE (*coming out of the kitchen*). David, here's your water. (*Crosses to* DAVID *with his drink.*)

SHEILA. Oh, Jane darling, Mr. Hoylake-Johnston won't want water.

DAVID. Oh, but I do.

SHEILA. Don't you drink, then?

DAVID. Very seldom.

SHEILA. Won't you have a cigarette?

DAVID. No, thank you—I don't smoke.

SHEILA. Indeed?

JANE. Oh, David, did I leave the tap on? Would you be an angel?

(DAVID *goes into the kitchen.*)

Mummy, go to bed. You're vulgar—you're so obvious.

SHEILA. But darling, he's—

JANE. He's not. He's sweet.

SHEILA. You don't know him.

JANE. I do.

DAVID (*coming back*). It wasn't on.

JANE. Oh, good! I'll get the biscuits. (*She goes out* R.)

(JIMMY *comes in* U.L.C.)

JIMMY. Sheila, come along, for heaven's sake!

SHEILA. I'm coming, darling. I've been seeing Mr. Hoylake-Johnston has got everything he wants.

(JIMMY *takes* SHEILA *by the arm.*)

Good night!

(*They go out* U.L.C. JANE *comes back* R. *with a plate of biscuits and a glass of milk.*)

JANE. Has Mummy gone?

DAVID. Yes. I hope she doesn't mind me doing this?

JANE. Oh, no!—we've lots of biscuits. (*Puts biscuits down on coffee table. Drinks.*)

(DAVID *laughs.*)

(*Sitting up* U.S. *end of sofa.*) Weren't you surprised when Mummy rang you up this morning?

DAVID. Yes—I was a bit.

JANE. I can't think why you came.

DAVID (*sits* U.S. *end of coffee table*). Oh, just for fun.

JANE. And have you had it?

DAVID. Well, I'm having it.

JANE. Oh, good! (*She drinks again.*)

DAVID. Are you?

JANE. Yes.

DAVID. Did you like the night-club?

JANE. Which one?

DAVID. All, or any of them?

JANE. Yes—I like this better, though.

DAVID. Yes, so do I.

JANE. Because we're alone—just you and I.

DAVID. And Mother, off and on!

JANE. Not now. She's gone to bed. (*Drinks again.*) I've only been to one once before, on my birthday.

DAVID. A night-club?

JANE. No—but you have, often, haven't you?
DAVID. Yes.
JANE. Thousands?
DAVID. Oh no—I hope not!
JANE. Hundreds, then?
DAVID. Perhaps.
JANE. With lots of girls?
DAVID. Oh, no—just one.
JANE. With one girl lots of times—or lots of girls just once?
DAVID. Well, anyway—not one girl lots of times. (*Empties glass.*)
JANE. Did you take Brenda Barrington out to a night-club ever?
DAVID. Yes.
JANE. How many times?
DAVID. I really can't remember—once or twice.
JANE. Another water? I'd like another milk.
DAVID. All right.

> (JANE *gets up, taking both glasses, and goes to the kitchen. She opens the door, and there is* JIMMY.)

JANE. Daddy! What are you doing?
JIMMY. Hullo, Jane! I'm filling up your mother's bottle.
JANE. I'll do it. Go and talk to David. (*Exit.*)

> (JIMMY *comes in.*)

JIMMY. Hullo, David!
DAVID. Hullo.
JIMMY (*crossing above sofa to door*). Don't get up. You getting all you want to drink?
DAVID. Yes—Jane's just getting me another glass.
JIMMY. What of?
DAVID. Of water.
JIMMY. Water! Do you really drink the stuff?
DAVID. Yes, frequently.
JIMMY. Have you got something wrong with you?
DAVID. No—not that I'm aware of.
JIMMY. Good. How's Jane for a dancing partner?
DAVID. Very good.
JIMMY. And her conversation?
DAVID. Sweet.
JIMMY. Oh, good! Has she been sweet to you?

DAVID. Yes, rather.

JIMMY. Good. I hope that you've been sweet to her—

DAVID. I hope so, too.

JIMMY. You shouldn't have gone off like that, alone. Her mother nearly had a fit. She thought—well, you know what she thought.

DAVID. I can imagine it.

JIMMY. I bet you can't imagine it as vividly as she can!

(JANE *comes in* R.)

JANE. It's boiling, Daddy. Here you are. (*Gives him the bottle.*)

JIMMY. Thanks.

JANE. Run along—or Mummy'll be screaming for you!

JIMMY. Yes, that's right. Well, good night—don't get up! (*He goes* U.L.C.)

(JANE *gives* DAVID *his water, then sits on sofa. There is a long pause while they drink.*)

DAVID. Well, I suppose I ought to go.

JANE. There's no need to. I'm not the least bit sleepy yet. Are you?

DAVID. No—not a bit.

JANE. That can't be very comfortable. Why don't you sit on this? It's lovely!

(JANE *moves* D.S., DAVID *sits* U.S. *end of sofa.*)

DAVID. All right.

JANE. I sleep here all day long.

DAVID. Oh, do you?

JANE. Yes—except when Mummy's dragging me round exhibitions, and dress shows and things.

DAVID. Does she do that?

JANE. Yes—nearly every day. She's educating me.

DAVID. Oh yes—I see.

JANE (*pause*). What would you like to do now?

DAVID. What would you?

JANE. I don't know. Yes, I do. I'd like to kiss you.

DAVID. Why?

JANE. Because I like you.

DAVID. Oh, do you kiss everybody that you like?

JANE. I don't like anybody, except you. There couldn't be a better reason, could there?

DAVID. No, I suppose not.

JANE. Well, can I?

DAVID. Well, yes, if you want to.

JANE. I do want to. Turn your face round. (*She kisses* DAVID.) Did I do it right?

DAVID. Very nicely.

JANE. Not so bad, considering it was the first time?

DAVID. Not so bad at all.

JANE. You weren't very good, though, were you?

DAVID. Wasn't I? I'm sorry.

JANE. No—you didn't seem to have your heart in it. Perhaps you didn't—when we started, anyhow.

DAVID. Not when we started—no.

JANE. But you were getting better when we finished. Would you like to try again?

DAVID. Yes, please. (*He does.*)

JANE. Oh, David—is that how you kissed—

(JIMMY *comes in* U.L.C.)

JIMMY. Jane, darling, your mother thinks . . . Oh, don't get up. (*To* JANE.) Your mother thinks you ought to go to bed.

JANE. Oh, she's a nuisance!

JIMMY. Yes, I know.

DAVID. I'd better go. Good night, Jane. Good night, Jimmy.

JIMMY. Good night, David.

(DAVID *goes out* U.L.C. *and the flat door shuts.*)

(*Pause.*) Well, I'll toddle back to bed. Night, Jane.

JANE. Night, Daddy.

(JIMMY *goes off down the passage. We hear his door shut.*
JANE *goes and collects stole and gloves. Turns out lights by kitchen door. Crosses to window, turning out fire as she passes it. Opens curtains and looks out. Moves back as* DAVID *enters.*)

JANE (*whispering*). David, darling!

DAVID (*whispering, too*). Your key!

JANE. Oh!

(DAVID *hands over the key.*)

DAVID. Well, good night!

JANE. Good night, David—

(*They are about to fall into each others arms.*)

JIMMY (*off in passage*). Yes, it is on all right, darling, I'll turn it out.

DAVID *and* JANE *spring apart.* JIMMY *comes in, without seeing them, and absent-mindedly flicks off the light; then he goes back to his room. They smile and embrace again.*

CURTAIN

SCENE 2

Breakfast time, the same day. There is a bouquet of flowers lying on the back of the sofa.

DAVID BULLOCH *is pacing up and down* U.L. *He is in full Guards uniform with a bearskin in one hand and a sword in the other. He sits on sofa as the telephone rings. After looking at it for some time, he rises to* L. *of telephone. Finding that he's unable to lift receiver because of sword, he places sword* R. *of telephone.*

BULLOCH (*at telephone*). Hullo? I dunno. I'll have a look. (*He looks at the dial number.*) Yes, it is. No, I'm not. Well, David Bulloch. Who? Oh, hullo, David. Well, I'm looking for my cigarette-case, actually. I left it here last night. So I came round to get it. No, I haven't actually. But I'm still hoping. No, she's not. I mean, she's still in bed. They all are, actually. At least, there's no one having breakfast yet. What? I say, steady on, old chap. I can't do that. I can't just barge in in my uniform. Well, we're rehearsing trooping the colour. No, sorry, David, it's not done. I'll take a message, if you like. All right, then you'd better ring again. (*He puts down the telephone and resumes his seat on sofa.*)

(JIMMY *enters* U.L.C., *partly dressed.* DAVID BULLOCH *stands up awkwardly.*)

Good morning, sir.

JIMMY (*looking round and shuddering*). Great Heavens, has war broken out?

BULLOCH. No, we're rehearsing for the trooping the colour.

JIMMY (*crossing to breakfast table*). Oh, good show.

BULLOCH (*looking at his watch*). At ten.

JIMMY (*looking at his*). Good. Have some breakfast?

BULLOCH. No, thanks. I've had mine.

JIMMY. Oh, good. (*Offers* BULLOCH *the* Express.) Would you like to read the *Express* while I have mine?

BULLOCH. No, thanks. (U.C. *between sofa and rostrum.*) Could I see Jane, sir?

JIMMY. I don't think that she's awake yet.

BULLOCH. Oh dear, and I'm on parade at ten.

JIMMY. Yes, so you said. (*Goes to trolley for coffee pot and milk jug.*)

> (*During pause* JIMMY *returns to the table with coffee and milk and pours himself out a cup.*)

BULLOCH. Sir, may I marry Jane, sir?

JIMMY. May you what?

BULLOCH. Sir, marry Jane, sir.

JIMMY. You'd better ask my wife. She deals with all that side. She'll be in in a minute.

BULLOCH. Oh, good. Thank you, sir.

> (JIMMY *stands watching* BULLOCH *as he walks away. Another pause.*)

JIMMY. Why don't you put that bird's nest down somewhere?

BULLOCH. Oh, right, sir. Thank you, sir. (*He puts down the bearskin on chair* D.R.C.)

JIMMY. Feel better?

BULLOCH. Yes, thank you, sir. (*Pause. Crosses below sofa.*) I haven't asked Jane yet.

JIMMY. Oh, haven't you? Well, that's important.

BULLOCH. Yes, I know it is. I tried to last night, but she wouldn't listen. Then she disappeared.

JIMMY. Indeed?

BULLOCH. That's why I rushed round here this morning.

JIMMY. Quite.

BULLOCH (*above sofa by fire*). I only hope it's not too late.

JIMMY. Too late? She's only seventeen.

BULLOCH. No—I mean David Hoylake-Johnston. He's—

> (*Enter* SHEILA U.L.C.)

JIMMY. Ah, Sheila, here you are. Here's David.

BULLOCH. Oh, good morning, Mrs. Broadbent.

SHEILA (*delighted*). David, what an early call! And what a pretty suit! I do hope Jimmy's given you some breakfast.

JIMMY. David hasn't come for breakfast. He wants to marry Jane. (*Sits in* L. *chair.*)

SHEILA (*to* BULLOCH). David, are you and Jane engaged?

BULLOCH. Well, no—I haven't asked her yet.

SHEILA. I'll go and get her.

JIMMY. Don't you ask her, Sheila. Leave all that to David.

SHEILA. Really, Jimmy, I'm not utterly half-witted! (*Going out* U.L.C., *shouting.*) Jane! It's David . . .

JIMMY. You were saying about David Hoylake-Johnston?

BULLOCH (*crosses to* JIMMY, *one foot on rostrum*). Yes, sir. I was going to say that he's a cad.

JIMMY. Oh, were you?

BULLOCH. Yes, well you know about Brenda Barrington and him?

JIMMY. Not officially, no.

BULLOCH. Good Lord. I thought that everybody knew about the weekend when Colonel Barrington found Brenda in his room.

JIMMY. In whose room?

BULLOCH. David Hoylake-Johnston's. In the middle of the night.

JIMMY. Indeed. What were they doing there?

BULLOCH (*turns away to arm of sofa*). Well, what do you expect? He gave her brandy.

JIMMY. Brandy—really?

BULLOCH. And nuts.

JIMMY. Nuts. Good Lord!

BULLOCH. Then, what with all the brandy and the nuts, it was a piece of cake.

JIMMY. What was?

BULLOCH. Well, surely you can guess.

JIMMY (*rising and coming round below table to edge of rostrum*). You must forgive me if I got confused with all these different foodstuffs. Do you mean that when the nuts were finished, and the brandy, Brenda, so to speak, was finished, too?

BULLOCH. That's right.

JIMMY. How do you know all this?

BULLOCH. Well, I was staying there.

JIMMY. Oh, were you? Were you really?

(SHEILA *comes in* U.L.C., *followed by a tidier* JANE.)

SHEILA. Here's Jane.

BULLOCH. Oh, hullo, Jane!

JANE. It's you! Oh, Lord! (*Crosses* D.S. *to* JIMMY *and kisses him good morning.*)

SHEILA (*crosses between* BULLOCH *and breakfast table to below sofa*). Jane, don't be rude!

JANE (*turns to* BULLOCH. JIMMY *returns to chair and sits*). Why are you dressed like that?

BULLOCH. Because I'm on parade at ten.

JANE (*looks at watch. Crosses to trolley*). Oh, good.

BULLOCH (*takes flowers from sofa*). I've brought you these— (*He holds out the flowers.*)

JANE (*crossing* D.S. *with coffee pot and milk jug, pours out cup. Puts coffee pot and milk jug on table*). What for?

BULLOCH. To give to you, of course.

JANE. Oh. (*She sits down.*) Sugar please, Daddy.

SHEILA. Darling, David's come to see you and he's in a hurry and it's rather special really.

JANE. What is?

SHEILA. David's visit. (*Crosses* U.S.C. *towards door.*) David will enlighten you.

JANE. Oh, don't slop, Mummy.

SHEILA. Well, it's high time that I went and dressed. Jimmy, it's getting late—you ought to go and shave.

JIMMY. I have. Oh, right. Yes, rather. Anybody like *The Times?* No?

SHEILA. No one wants it, Jimmy. Take it with you. Go on, dear. You always have for twenty years.

(*He goes and—after a smile, nauseating to* JANE—SHEILA *goes, too.* JANE *helps herself to egg from trolley, taking coffee pot and milk jug back with her.*)

BULLOCH (*grabs* JANE *from behind*). Jane, darling—

JANE. Go away. Your hands are cold. (BULLOCH *steps back.*) What do you think you're doing here at this hour in the morning?

BULLOCH. I came specially to see you.

JANE. Why on earth?

BULLOCH. Because I want to marry you.

JANE. Oh, don't be goofy!

BULLOCH. But I do.

JANE. Whatever for?

BULLOCH (*tries to hold* JANE's *hands, but his thumb slips into her plate of egg*). Because I love you.

JANE (*moves away from* BULLOCH *and sits* D.S. *chair. Starts to eat*). Oh, since when?

BULLOCH. Two nights ago—

JANE. You've got a funny way of showing it.

BULLOCH. What do you mean?

JANE. Attacking me last night, when I was telephoning.

BULLOCH (*coming* D.L. *of table to* JANE). You aren't telephoning now.

JANE. I'm eating scrambled eggs. That's just as bad.

BULLOCH. Does that mean I can kiss you, when you've finished?

JANE. No, it doesn't.

BULLOCH. Please, Jane. (*Tries to get her hand again.*) I'm in love with you.

JANE. You've said that once.

BULLOCH. Well, then—

JANE. Well, then—I'm not in love with you.

BULLOCH. Then who are you in love with?

JANE. Nobody.

BULLOCH (*slightly away from her*). You're lying. You're in love with David Hoylake-Johnston.

JANE. Don't be silly.

BULLOCH. Well, who then?

JANE. With nobody, I said.

BULLOCH (*crossing below table to* C.). I don't believe you. I'm in love with someone all the time.

JANE. Then you're over-sexed.

BULLOCH (*turning to her*). Well, I can't help it if I am.

JANE. I'm sorry—I can't either.

BULLOCH (*goes down on one knee, takes her hand*). But you've got to—

JANE. David, go away.

BULLOCH. I won't. I've got to kiss you. I'll go mad if I don't, Jane. I will. I've felt so awful ever since I've wanted to. I think I've got a temperature.

JANE. Well then, you shouldn't go on parade. Shall I ask Mummy for her clinical thermometer?

BULLOCH. No, please don't. Please, Jane, I do love you.

JANE. David! That's three times.

R.D.—E

BULLOCH. I can't help that. (*Bringing* JANE *to her feet. Both struggling.*)
Come here, Jane—Jane.

JANE. How can you in the morning, David? David—leave go—David,
I'll call Mummy if you don't. I'll scream if you don't let me go.

BULLOCH. Well, call her then. I just don't care.

JANE. Mummy—Mummy—Mummy!

(SHEILA *rushes in* U.L.C.)

SHEILA. Yes, darling? Here I am.

JANE (*running to her*). Oh, Mummy.

SHEILA (*misunderstanding the calling*). There, there, darling. (*She drops*
JANE.) David— (*To* DAVID.) dearest boy.

JANE. Oh, Mummy, don't be silly. It's not on.

SHEILA (*turns back to* JANE). What isn't on?—But, darling, I thought
David asked you—

JANE. So he did—

SHEILA. And you said no?

JANE. That's right.

SHEILA. But, darling, why?

BULLOCH (*interrupting*). I say, I really ought to go.

(JANE *goes and closes kitchen door.*)

SHEILA. Must you really? Oh, David, I'm so sorry.

BULLOCH. Good-bye, Mrs. Broadbent. Good-bye, Jane.

JANE. Good-bye. (*Crossing to breakfast table.*)

BULLOCH (*picking up bearskin*). I hope we'll meet again. (*He turns to
go.*)

SHEILA. Of course you will. Tonight, at Susan Shelly's dance!

BULLOCH. Oh, good.

SHEILA. You wouldn't dine with us?

JANE. Oh, Mummy—honestly—

SHEILA. But we've got no one else.

JANE. If David comes then I won't go.

SHEILA. How can you be so petty, Jane?

JANE. I mean it.

SHEILA. I'm so sorry, David.

BULLOCH (*picks up flowers, goes to door*). That's all right. Good-bye,
Mrs. Broadbent—

(*Feeling something missing, he looks round and* SHEILA *sees his
sword and hands it to him. He goes* U.L.C.)

SHEILA (*crossing to table and picking up cup and saucer, she goes to trolley and pours out coffee).* Why must you be so utterly unreasonable? We've got nobody to dine tonight.

JANE. I'd rather that than Goofy.

SHEILA. You're selfish, that's what's wrong with you. You never seem to think of all the work I have to do to get a dinner-partner for you— (*Sits U.S. place with cup of coffee.*)

JANE. Please don't bother, Mummy, I can get my own.

SHEILA. Who? David Hoylake-Johnston, I suppose!

JANE. Why not?

SHEILA. Because he's undesirable.

JANE. He's not.

(*Enter* JIMMY U.L.C.)

JIMMY. I heard a lot of shouting. Anybody hurt?

JANE. No, Goofy's gone, that's all.

JIMMY (*crossing D.C. with* The Times). Oh, good.

SHEILA. What do you mean, "oh good"?

JIMMY. Well, good for us and good for Jane.

SHEILA. It isn't good for Jane.

JANE. Oh, Mummy, be your age. I couldn't love him less.

SHEILA. Love. You're talking like a school-girl. Love, indeed! What do you know of love?

JANE. A lot more than you think.

SHEILA. What do you mean?

JANE. Exactly what I say.

JIMMY (*reading* The Times). Hullo, the Duke of Positano's dead.

SHEILA. Who cares?

JIMMY. The Duchess, probably. Oh no, she's dead as well.

SHEILA. Jimmy, please stop reading that newspaper.

JIMMY. I'm sorry, but it's very interesting. It says he's been succeeded, through the female line, by—

SHEILA. Oh, for heaven's sake stop going on about the Duke of Positano.

JIMMY. Sorry, darling, but I thought you'd be interested.

SHEILA. I couldn't be less interested.

JIMMY. In that case I'll stop reading. What's the matter?

JANE. Nothing, Daddy. I'm in love, that's all.

JIMMY (*crossing front of sofa*). Bad luck.

JANE. It's not bad luck. I love him terribly.

JIMMY. Who?

JANE. David.

JIMMY (*sits on sofa*). David. But I thought you'd given him the push.

JANE. No. David Hoylake-Johnston.

JIMMY. Oh.

SHEILA. It's no use sitting there and saying "oh".

JIMMY. Oh, isn't it?

SHEILA. How can you be so babyish? To get infatuated with a man like that.

JANE. It's not infatuation, Mummy. That's what David Bulloch's got for me. But mine for David Hoylake-Johnston's love.

SHEILA (*rising and crossing R. to wastepaper basket. Tears up envelope and puts card on shelf with the others*). I never heard such nonsense. You'll be saying next that he's in love with you.

JANE. I think he is.

SHEILA. How can you be so silly? Give me just one reason why he should be.

JANE. I could give you many more than that but I'd rather keep them to myself. (*She has a beatific smile on her face.*)

SHEILA (*suspicious. Crossing back to table and sitting*). Were you at Zizzi's all the time last night—from when you left the dance until you came back here?

JANE. Yes, Mummy.

SHEILA. You went nowhere else at all?

JANE. No, Mummy, we were dancing almost non-stop. Why should we go somewhere else? (*Rises, crossing U.C. between* JIMMY *and* SHEILA.)

SHEILA. Your father thought he might have taken you back to his flat.

JIMMY. I—

JANE. Daddy, but whatever for?

JIMMY. You'd better ask your mother, Jane.

JANE. Mummy, whatever for? (*Wide-eyed.*) I mean to say, what's his flat got that this one hasn't got?

SHEILA. I've never seen it, I'm happy to say, so I couldn't tell you.

JANE. Well, I'm sure it isn't half as comfortable.

SHEILA. Jimmy, can't you say something to her?

JIMMY. What? Yes, rather. Oh yes, by the way, you left the light on.

JANE. When?

JIMMY. Last night.

JANE. Where?

JIMMY. In here.

JANE. I'm sorry, Daddy.

JIMMY. That's all right. I came along and turned it out.

JANE. I know.

JIMMY. How do you know?

JANE. Well, it's not on now.

JIMMY. Now, say you're sorry to your mother.

JANE (*crossing below sofa to* U.S.R. *chair and sitting*). But I'm not. I won't be blamed for something that I'm not to blame for. Mummy introduced me to him, after all.

JIMMY. That's fair enough.

SHEILA (*rounding on* JIMMY). So it's my fault?

JIMMY. I never said so, darling.

SHEILA. You implied it, though.

JIMMY. Well, if it isn't yours initially, whose is it?

SHEILA. Yours!

JIMMY. Mine? I like that. Now how on earth could it be mine?

SHEILA. It's in your family.

JIMMY. What is?

SHEILA. That sort of thing.

JIMMY. (*rising*). What sort of thing?

SHEILA. She's bred for it.

JIMMY. Don't talk about me as if I were a horse.

> (JANE, *seeing that the storm is diverted from her own head for the moment, carries on unconcernedly with her breakfast.*)

SHEILA. Of course, I never should have married you, with all that rotten Broadbent blood.

JIMMY (*crossing round* D.S. *arm of sofa up to shelf. Cleans glasses*). My blood's all right.

SHEILA. How can you say that, Jimmy? (*Rises and crosses to trolley with cup for more coffee.*) What about your sister Rose?

JIMMY. Be careful, Sheila. I'm extremely fond of Rose.

SHEILA. Of course, men always are.

JIMMY. Oh, Sheila, shut up, will you?

SHEILA. And then your Uncle Richard. Look at him!

JIMMY (*crossing* L. *behind sofa*). How can I look at him, he's dead!

SHEILA. What about cousin Alec—living in Algiers, pretending that he paints.

JIMMY. Your family's above suspicion, I suppose?

SHEILA (*sits* U.S. *chair at table*). It's not as bad as yours, I'm happy to say.

JIMMY (*moving below sofa*). Oh, isn't it? You're not forgetting brother Harold, are you?—Asked to leave his regiment.

SHEILA. That's not fair. You know quite well he asked to leave.

JIMMY (*turns to her*). He didn't have to ask 'em twice, though, did he?

SHEILA. Now, Jimmy, how could Harold help it if the silly little woman fell in love with him?

JIMMY. Quite easily—according to Arbelle.

SHEILA. Arbelle—she doesn't understand him. How he ever married her's beyond me.

JIMMY. Yes, it was unlike him, wasn't it? Except that he was broke!

SHEILA. Are you implying Harold married Arbelle for her money, Jimmy?

JIMMY. Well, she couldn't very well have married him for his.

SHEILA (*rises*). What do you mean by that?

JIMMY. Nothing, darling. Your father told me he'd paid up for Harold seven times.

SHEILA. Father exaggerates. You must know that by now.

JIMMY. Well, you've got that in common, anyway.

SHEILA. What do you mean by "anyway"? (*They meet* C., SHEILA *on rostrum*.)

JIMMY. Oh, nothing.

SHEILA. Jimmy.

JIMMY. Darling, I just meant you weren't very like your father. I'm not sorry. I prefer you as you are.

(SHEILA *kicks his ankle and runs out of the room*.)   .

(U.S. *behind sofa*.) She kicked me!

JANE. How simply fascinating knowing what I got born into after all these years.

(*The telephone rings.* JIMMY *goes to it*.)

JIMMY (*at telephone*). Hullo—yes. Yes, it is. Hold on. I'll get her. Jane, for you.

JANE. Who is it, Daddy?

JIMMY. David.

JANE. David which?

JIMMY. You'd better ask him: he should know.

(JIMMY, *humming a tune, crosses* U.R. *to pick up his brief-case. Then below sofa to table where he picks up some letters, which he puts into his brief-case*.)

JANE. Hullo? Who is it? David? Oh, David, it's you! Hullo! Yes. Very well. And how are you? Oh, good! But I'm not dressed yet. David, you are awful. All right. But you mustn't mind if I'm still having breakfast. What? Oh, David, don't be silly! (*She giggles and hangs up. Coming* D.S. *toward* JIMMY.) That was David, Daddy.

JIMMY. Thanks for taking me into your confidence.

JANE. He's coming round.

JIMMY. Not David Bulloch, I presume?

JANE. No fear. Do you like David Hoylake-Johnston, Daddy?

JIMMY. Yes, your mother doesn't, though. I hope she won't be rude to him this morning. She's rather overwrought.

JANE. I expect it's just a hang-over.

JIMMY. It's more than that. It's David Hoylake-Johnston's reputation.

JANE. Daddy, honestly—to have this hate against poor David just because he slipped up once—

JIMMY. Was it once?

JANE. Well, it was once, wasn't it?

JIMMY. Yes, so one hopes.

JANE. You'd think that Mummy didn't know a thing! You ought to educate her, Daddy.

JIMMY (*sits chair* D.L.C.). In what way?

JANE. Well, every young man does that sort of thing provided that he gets the opportunity.

JIMMY. Indeed?

JANE. Or didn't they do things like that in your day?

JIMMY. Are you speaking generally, or are you asking me a question?

JANE (*kneels in front of him*). Daddy, who was the first woman you made love to?

JIMMY. Sylvia O'Brien.

JANE. Daddy, who was she?

JIMMY. The Vicar's daughter in our village.

JANE. Was she beautiful?

JIMMY. No—striking is the word.

JANE. And did you kiss her?

JIMMY. Certainly.

JANE. Where?

JIMMY. In the usual place—somewhere around the mouth.

JANE. No, Daddy—don't be silly! I mean whereabouts? The garden or—the river? You know what I mean?

JIMMY. I kissed her in the graveyard after evensong.

JANE. Oh, Daddy, what a rip you were! How old were you?

JIMMY. Thirteen—and she was nine.

JANE. What happened to her?

JIMMY. She went home to tea.

JANE. No, afterwards, I mean?

JIMMY. She joined the A.T.S. when she grew up. I met her in the war, in Worthing.

JANE. Did you kiss her then?

JIMMY. No! Just inspected her.

JANE. Daddy, what do you mean?

JIMMY. Exactly what I say. I met her on parade. She had a ladder in her stocking.

JANE. Did you tell her?

JIMMY. No. I think she knew.

JANE. But when did you make love to someone properly?

JIMMY (turns away from her). Oh, some years later.

JANE. What was her name?

JIMMY. Solange.

JANE. Solange!

JIMMY. She was French.

JANE. And where did you make love to Solange, Daddy?

JIMMY. At a house in Paris.

JANE. Her own home?

JIMMY. No—not exactly—she was working there.

JANE. You mean she was a maid?

JIMMY. No, not exactly.

JANE. Well, what was she doing there?

JIMMY. Oh, this and that.

JANE. Oh, Daddy, aren't you wicked? You're just as bad as David! And then you met Mummy?

JIMMY. Yes.

JANE. And did you kiss her?

JIMMY. Ultimately.

JANE. And that's why I'm here. Oh, isn't life extraordinary?

JIMMY. Yes, I suppose so when you look at it like that.

JANE (kneels up and hugs him). Oh, Daddy, I do love you. What I'd do without you, I don't know.

JIMMY. Me?

JANE. Yes. Because you are on my side, aren't you, Daddy?

JIMMY. I've not said so.

JANE. No, I know. But then you can't—because you can't go against Mummy and convention. I can understand all that.

JIMMY. That's most broadminded of you.

JANE. Not a bit. It's elementary. I know you've got to bluff it out with Mummy to the end. But, actually, let's face it, from the moment you met that French girl you'd had it as a moralist.

(MRS. EDGAR *enters* U.L.C.)

MRS. EDGAR. Mr. Hoylake-Johnston, sir.

(*Enter* DAVID. JANE *rises to meet him.*)

JIMMY. Good morning, David. (*Rises below chair. Turns round the back of it.*)

DAVID. Hullo, Jimmy. Hullo, Jane. I've brought you these. (*He holds out a bouquet of flowers.*)

JANE. Oh, darling David, they're simply lovely. (*She falls into his arms.*)

JIMMY. Well, I suppose I'd better go and have another shave?

(JIMMY *goes out. They smile after him.*)

JANE. Oh, David darling, it seems ages since you went away.

DAVID. It's only three hours actually.

JANE. I know, but doesn't it seem years?

DAVID (*crosses above sofa*). Er yes . . . Jane, what was David Bulloch doing here?

JANE. Who told you he was here? (*Puts flowers on sofa.*)

DAVID. I rang up earlier. He answered.

JANE. Oh.

DAVID (D.R.). He said he came to get his cigarette case.

JANE. Oh.

DAVID. I don't believe it, though. (*Turns up to* JANE.) What did he want?

JANE. Oh, nothing much. Just me.

DAVID. You. Do you mean that he proposed to you?

JANE. That's right.

DAVID. Good heavens! What infernal cheek. Jane . . . (*Turns away from* JANE R.) I've got something to tell you, darling.

JANE (*moving towards him*). That's all right, my darling. I already know, and I don't mind.

DAVID. Oh, so you've seen *The Times*?

JANE. It isn't in the paper, is it?

DAVID. Yes, this morning.

JANE. Do you mean she's suing you?

DAVID. What are you talking about?

JANE. Brenda Barrington, of course.

DAVID (*laughing*). Oh, don't be silly.

JANE. Well, what is it?

DAVID. My great-uncle's died.

JANE. Oh, poor, poor you. I'm sure you loved him terribly.

DAVID (*crosses* L. *in front of* JANE). I never met him actually. He was Italian. My mother's uncle. He was very rich. (*Turns to her.*) And I'm his heir. It's through the female line. So I'm not David Hoylake-Johnston any more.

JANE. Who are you then?

DAVID. The Duke of Positano. Do you mind?

JANE. No. Ought I to?

DAVID. It means I'd have to live there half the time.

JANE. Oh, darling.

DAVID. Have you ever been to Italy?

JANE. Yes. Florence, once, with Daddy.

DAVID. Well, that's where I'll live. I've got a sort of palace there.

JANE. What do you mean, "a sort of palace"?

DAVID. Well, it is a palace, actually. It's much too big to live in.

JANE. Oh.

DAVID. But there's a villa on Capri.

JANE. Oh, David darling, what a lot of housekeeping.

DAVID. Oh, darling, I can't tell you how relieved I am you've taken it so well.

(*They embrace.*)

Jane, darling—

JANE. Yes?

DAVID. You wouldn't—?

    (SHEILA *comes in* U.L.C. *and finds them in each others arms. They break as* DAVID *sees her.*)

Oh, good morning, Mrs. Broadbent.

SHEILA. Jane.

JANE. Yes, Mummy.

SHEILA. What on earth is Mr. Hoylake-Johnston doing?

JANE (*lamely*). Giving me some flowers.

SHEILA. Jane, leave the room. At once. At once, I said.

JANE (*crossing to* SHEILA). But, Mummy, David's come to see me.

DAVID (*master of the situation*). Go on, Jane. I'll wait.

(JANE *kisses* DAVID *again and, picking up the flowers, she goes out* U.L.C.)

SHEILA. Now, Mr. Hoylake-Johnston, please explain yourself. What are you doing here?

DAVID. I came to give Jane some flowers. And I was hoping you'd let me take her out to Susan Shelley's dance tonight.

SHEILA. I'm sorry, Mr. Hoylake-Johnston, Jane's already going out.

DAVID. Oh, but I thought she said last night—

SHEILA. What Jane said last night is not important. What's important is what I am saying now. Will you be kind enough to leave this flat?

DAVID. But I told Jane I'd wait.

SHEILA. Please, Mr. Hoylake-Johnston.

DAVID. I'm sorry, Mrs. Broadbent, but I said I'd wait.

SHEILA. I see. In that case, I'm afraid I'll have to ask my husband to remove you. (*Opens door* U.L.C. *and calls off stage.*) Jimmy. Jimmy!

JIMMY (*off*). Hullo, darling.

SHEILA (*calling*). Would you come here a minute please?

JIMMY (*off*). Right, darling.

SHEILA (*comes back into room*). He won't be a minute.

DAVID. Oh, thank you.

(*There is a long pause.*)

SHEILA (*goes back to doorway and calls*). Jimmy!

JIMMY (*off*). Coming, darling.

(*There is another pause, then the sound of water flushing.* SHEILA *still stands waiting.* JIMMY *comes in.*)

Hullo, darling. What's the matter?

SHEILA. Everything. I came in here and found Jane in this young man's arms.

JIMMY. I say!

SHEILA. And now he has refused point-blank to leave the flat.

JIMMY. Oh.

SHEILA. Will you please remove him, Jimmy?

JIMMY (*looking nervously at* DAVID). Better chuck him out, eh?

SHEILA. Well, then, come along.

JIMMY. You'd better go, my dear. It may not be too nice to watch.

SHEILA (*running to him*). Take care of yourself.

JIMMY. Yes, darling.

(SHEILA *goes off* U.L.C., *he looks after her bravely.*

Turning to HOYLAKE-JOHNSTON *and, by mistake, moving towards him.*)
Well, I'm sorry.

DAVID (*aggressively*). You'll be sorrier if you start anything.

JIMMY (*deprecatingly*). No, no, I mean I'm sorry about your great-uncle. How old was he?

DAVID. Ninety-five.

JIMMY. Oh, asking for it, wasn't he?

SHEILA (*off, shouting*). Jimmy, are you all right?

JIMMY (*shouting*). Yes, darling. (*To* DAVID.) We'd better make a show. (*Both at door, with door open slightly, speaking loudly.*) Now look here, young fellow—

DAVID (*loudly*). Yes, I'm looking, Broadbent—

JIMMY (*loudly*). If you aren't out of here in two minutes, I'll chuck you out.

DAVID (*loudly*). Right, have a try.

JIMMY. That gives us two minutes. (DAVID *sits on sofa.*) Now then, are you in love with Jane?

DAVID. Yes?

JIMMY (*crossing* R.U.S. *of sofa*). Want to marry her?

DAVID. Of course.

JIMMY (U.R.) So much for the future, pretty rosy-looking, if it wasn't for the past. But what about that lost weekend when brandy flowed like water and poor Brenda Barrington's morale was cracking with the nuts?

DAVID. Who on earth told you that?

JIMMY. Never mind who told me. Not a very pretty story, is it?

DAVID. Not a very true one either.

JIMMY. Isn't it? I'm not surprised. Now if it'd been champagne and caviare.

DAVID. Oh, it was brandy, actually. I had some in my suitcase.

JIMMY. Was your suitcase full of nuts as well?

DAVID. No. They were Colonel Barrington's.

JIMMY. What?

(*Pause.*)

DAVID (*rising and crossing* L.). I can see I'll have to tell you.

JIMMY. Yes, I think you'd better.

DAVID. Well then, David Bulloch and I stayed a weekend with the Barringtons in May. Well, after we'd gone to bed on Sunday night, I had a damn good book.

JIMMY. What was it? I've not read a damn good book for years.

DAVID. "The Wilder Shores of Love".

JIMMY. I must remember that.

DAVID. Well I was reading happily just after one, when Brenda Barrington came rushing in and said that David Bulloch had attacked her in her room.

JIMMY. Why did she come to you?

DAVID. Because I was next door, and she was frightened. Well, she started crying, so I got the brandy out. Well, it worked wonders. She stopped crying. And then suddenly she said that she was hungry and would I go down and get her something from the kitchen. Well, I couldn't find the lights, and so I groped around for a bit, then I suddenly hit my knuckles on a plate of nuts that we'd had at dinner, and I took them up. Well, when I got back to my room the flask was lying empty on the floor, and Brenda Barrington was lying on the bed.

JIMMY. Not empty!

DAVID. No. Well, I suppose I must have made a noise . . .

JIMMY. Lie down.

DAVID. I beg your pardon?

JIMMY. Lie down. I think I hear Sheila. (DAVID *lies behind the coffee table with his head on it.* JIMMY *crosses to door.*) Not yet, darling. You wouldn't like it. (*Shuts door and returns to sofa.*) Carry on.

DAVID. Well, as I was saying, I must have made a noise downstairs, because the next thing that I knew was Colonel Barrington was standing in the doorway in a dreadful, yellow dressing gown accusing me of playing fast and loose with Brenda.

JIMMY. I say. Then what happened?

DAVID. Nothing. He just pointed at my suitcase and said "pack".

JIMMY. What did you do?

DAVID. I packed and drove straight back to London. Then next morning Brenda rang me up and said that she was being taken off to Switzerland by her mother in the afternoon. And that she hadn't told her father about David Bulloch because that'd make it look as if she made a habit of it and anyway he might have made her marry him, whereas she knew he wouldn't make her marry me.

JIMMY. So you accepted being thought a cad?

DAVID. Well, what else could I do? The evidence was circumstantial.

JIMMY. I should say it was.

DAVID (*rises and straightens hair*). That's all, except that David Bulloch naturally seized his chance and spread the story round to Mabel Crosswaite and of course I'd had it then.

JIMMY. Of course. And do you realize that Mabel knows about your escapade last night, which means that Jane'll get a reputation just like Brenda Barrington?

DAVID. We're getting married, so it doesn't matter.

JIMMY. Are you?

DAVID. Yes, with your permission.

JIMMY. My permission. You can have that any time you like. Then I can cancel that damn dance, and save myself a thousand quid.

DAVID. Well then?

JIMMY. But I don't sign the permits round here. My wife does that. And as things stand at present you two haven't got a hope of getting married, unless you are prepared to tell her what you've just told me.

DAVID. Would she believe it?

JIMMY. Of course not. In her eyes, the Bulloch boy can do no wrong.

DAVID. Then what am I to do?

JIMMY (rises). There's only one thing for it. You'll have to give up seeing Jane.

DAVID. I can't.

(DAVID paces D.S. JIMMY goes U.S.)

JIMMY. Then what do you suggest?

DAVID. I wish I knew.

(They stop.)

JIMMY. Of course, she doesn't know that you're the Duke of Positano.

DAVID. Would that bring her round?

JIMMY. It might.

DAVID. You mean that she's a—

JIMMY. Aren't we all?

DAVID. Let's tell her then.

JIMMY. No. We can't face her with it, just like that. Her prestige is at stake. We've got to let her do it on her own, somehow. (He clicks his fingers.) I've got it. (Crosses to DAVID above sofa, pushing him towards door as he talks.) Leave it all to me. Where are you going now?

DAVID. I wouldn't know.

JIMMY. Well, go to Black's. And get there at the double and keep near the telephone.

SHEILA (off). Jimmy, are you all right?

JIMMY. Yes, darling.

(*After a mock struggle, during which* JIMMY *drops an ashtray on the floor, they shake hands and* DAVID *goes out.* JIMMY *throws the sofa cushions on the floor.* SHEILA *comes in.*)

SHEILA (*goes to* JIMMY *and helps him to chair* U.S. *of breakfast table*). Jimmy, are you all right?

JIMMY (*staggering a bit*). Yes, darling.

SHEILA. Jimmy, I admire you so.

JIMMY. Oh, it was nothing.

(*The telephone rings and* SHEILA *goes to it.*)

SHEILA. Hullo. Yes? Oh, hullo, Mabel. What's that? Did he really? Red carnations. How too lovely. And he's taking her to Susan Shelley's dance. How lovely for her.

(JIMMY *grins to himself as he crosses* D.R. *to mirror, putting on jacket.*)

Who's Jane going with? (*Lying.*) Oh, a great friend. You'll see tonight. Well, goodbye, Mabel—I must rush. (*She hangs up.*) Oh, Jimmy, David Bulloch's taking out Clarissa.

JIMMY. Two nights running—well, I never! Mabel'll soon be getting his telephone number by heart.

SHEILA (*sits in chair* U.R.). Oh, Jimmy, it's been all my fault. If I'd let things be, Jane might have married him.

JIMMY. She's well out of that, if you ask me.

SHEILA. But that lovely place in Warwickshire.

JIMMY. It isn't lovely. It's riddled with dry rot.

SHEILA (*hopefully*). You mean it's crumbling?

JIMMY. Yes, nearly derelict.

SHEILA. Oh, Jimmy, you're so sweet to me. You mean I haven't spoilt her life?

JIMMY. Not yet.

SHEILA. But don't you see, when Mabel spreads the story round about last night, she'll lose her reputation.

JIMMY. Very probably.

SHEILA. And that means no more invitations.

JIMMY. Nonsense, she'll get plenty when the word gets round.

SHEILA. What word?

JIMMY. That she's worth taking out.

SHEILA. Jimmy!

JIMMY. Darling, you asked me yesterday what the young men wanted. Now you know. (*Kisses her and gets his dispatch case. Crossing* L. *towards door.*) Well, what's the orders for tonight?

SHEILA (*profoundly depressed*). Oh, drinks at seven. Then dinner for Susan Shelley's dance. I've no one to dine—I must have someone tonight.

JIMMY. What, after all that we've been through?

SHEILA. Yes, even after that.

JIMMY. You're game, I'll give you that.

SHEILA. Well, who am I to get?

(JANE *rushes in* U.L.C.)

JANE (*on rostrum* L. *of* JIMMY). Where's David?

SHEILA. Mr. Hoylake-Johnston's gone.

JANE. Gone! But he said he'd wait.

SHEILA. We didn't let him wait. Your father put him out. We both decided that he's undesirable and that you mustn't see him any more.

JANE. You haven't, have you, Daddy? It's all Mummy, isn't it?

SHEILA. Now, listen to me, Jane. Consider yourself lucky that I'm not like Mrs. Barrington. Consider yourself lucky that your father and I haven't packed you off home by the ten-fifteen. We haven't though. We've both decided that you've been a victim of infatuation, and of inexperience, and that therefore it's our duty to stand by you. In fact, when you rushed in here just now and rudely interrupted us, we happened to be on the point of fixing up a dinner-party for you tonight.

(JANE *bursts into tears and sits on chair* D.S.L. JIMMY *goes out* U.L.C. *to get his hat and umbrella.*)

I'm sorry, darling, but I am your mother and I do know what's best for you, honestly I do. I know I asked him in the first place, but that wasn't my fault—it was Mabel's. She deliberately gave me the wrong number as she wanted David Bulloch for Clarissa. Do stop crying, darling. Where's your handkerchief?

JANE. Haven't got one.

SHEILA. Well, have mine, darling. (*She wipes* JANE's *eyes.*) There, dry your eyes. Darling, please believe me. (*Crosses* R.) He's really not a very nice young man. Good-looking and attractive, yes— but he's not very nice. And you'll forget him in a day or two. I know you will. Now, dry your eyes again and help me think of someone for tonight. We'll put our heads together and get someone really nice—

(JIMMY *comes in again* U.L.C.)

Now, Jimmy, have you thought of anybody?

JIMMY. Why not try the Duke of Positano?

SHEILA. Who on earth's the Duke of Positano?

JIMMY. His great-uncle's died, according to my paper, and they've given his address as Black's. He's twenty-six, they say.

SHEILA. Oh, Jimmy, do you know him?

JIMMY. Might have played bridge with him, I shouldn't wonder, but apart from that—

SHEILA (*excitedly*). Jimmy, will he be at Black's now?

JIMMY (*surreptitiously looking at his watch*). With a bit of luck.

SHEILA. Please ring him for me, Jimmy.

JIMMY. No, no. I'm in a hurry. It'd come much better from you.

SHEILA. Well, what's the number?

JIMMY. Whitehall 8688.

(JANE *smiles.*)

SHEILA (*while dialling*). That's right, darling. You're being very brave. We only want you to be happy, darling. Don't we, Jimmy?

JIMMY. Yes.

SHEILA (*at telephone*). Hullo, is that Black's? Oh, is the Duke of Positano in, by any chance? It's Mrs. Broadbent speaking. Please. (*To the others.*) He's just come in.

(JIMMY *winks at* JANE, *and goes out* U.L.C.)

(*Brings telephone down to back of sofa. At telephone.*) Hullo, is that the Duke of Positano? Oh, good morning. Isn't it a lovely day? My name is Sheila Broadbent. I don't think you know me, but my husband's Jimmy Broadbent, who's a member of your Club. I'm quite sure that you've met him playing bridge or something. Well, it's the most awful cheek of me to ask you, but I wondered if you'd come and dine tonight for Susan Shelley's dance. Oh, just my husband and myself and Jane—our daughter—she's come out this year. You will come? (*To* JANE.) My dear, he sounds heavenly. (*At telephone.*) Oh, how charming. Well, then, sevenish for seven-thirty, fourteen Victor Court, the Sloane Square end of Eaton Square. At seven-thirty. Well, till then.

During the last few lines of the conversation the CURTAIN *slowly falls.*

FURNITURE PLOT

Above radiator shelf, over fire:
Small clock.
Large picture.

DOOR FURNITURE

Glass off stage. China on stage:
Two pair of china door handles.
One pair china finger plates, key-hole covers.
One pair glass finger plates, key-hole covers.
Two other door handles.
Pair two-switch plates.

ACT I SCENE I

PROPERTY PLOT

SET

Small chair.
Elbow chair with two cushions.
Brief-case.
Sofa with three cushions.
> *On the back: The Times.*
> *By* U.S. *arm:* wastepaper basket.
Long coffee table, with:
> Magazines.
> Cigarette box.
> Lighter.
> Matches.
> Ashtray.
Small kidney table.
> *First shelf:* ashtray.
> *Second shelf:* cigarette box, matches.
Small upholstered chair with no arms. One cushion.
Round table with false top set for breakfast.
> 1, 2, 3, chairs. 1, with *Telegraph* on back. 3, with *Express* on back.
Radiogram: record "Oh" by Pee Wee Hunt set ready.
Small stool. Pile of records on top.
Electric trolley, with:
> Coffee pot.
> Milk jug.
> Two plates.
> Dish of scrambled eggs.
> Serving spoon and fork.
Electric fire.
Indian rug.
Drinks cupboard.
> *First shelf:* bottle of gin, and other bottles.
> *Second shelf:* measuring glass, and other glasses.
> *Third shelf:* glasses.
Telephone with very long flex.

On first shelf under telephone: message pad and pencil. Magazines.
On bottom shelf: Set of telephone directories. Some other books.

SET

On radiator shelf above fire:
    Invitation cards.
    Notebook and pencil.
On radiator shelf L. *of fire:*
    Open cigarette box.
    A bottle of lens cleaning liquid, and a small piece of chamois leather.
On radiator shelf under drinks cupboard:
    Bowl of fruit.
    Large ashtray.
    Pair of ear-rings behind bowl.
    Pair of ear-rings behind ashtray.
False top for table set with:
    Tablecloth.
    First place: knife, fork, and small knife. Cup, saucer, and teaspoon.
    Side plate, and napkin. Five invitations in envelopes.
    Second place: knife, fork, and small knife. Cup, saucer, and teaspoon.
    Side plate, and napkin. Business letters, phone bill. Glass of orange.
    Plate with poached egg.
    Third place: knife, fork, and small knife. Cup, saucer, and teaspoon.
    Side plate, and napkin. Two letters. Glass of orange. Sugar in basin.
    Salt and pepper. Toast in rack. Butter dish and knife.
Off R. *in kitchen for scene change:*
    Tray set with:
    Eight cocktail glasses.
    Swizzle sticks.
    Bottle of vermouth.
    Whisky decanter.
    Sherry decanter.
    Soda syphon.
    Cocktail shaker and napkin.

AND

    Tray set with:
    Ashtray.
    Ice bucket.
    Dish of cherries on sticks.
    Bowl of nuts.
    Two plates of small eats.

PERSONAL

    JIMMY: glasses, and empty cigarette case.

ACT I Scene 2

STRIKE

    The false top from round table.

Chair No. 1.
Trolley.
Wastepaper basket.

RE–SET

Round table to back into windows.
Chair Nos. 2 and 3 to either side.
Stool to c. of rostrum.
Cigarette box and matches, to top shelf of sofa table.
To original place:
Telephone from small sofa table.
Telephone book from back of sofa.
Who's Who from coffee table.

SET

Drinks tray on round table in window.
Ice bucket, cherries, food, ashtray and nuts on round table.
Close u.s. window.
Tidy cushions.
Bedroom door open.
L.C. door open.

ACT II SCENE 1

STRIKE

Two glasses from coffee table.
One glass, bowl of nuts and plate of eats from radiator shelf.
Cocktail shaker from under drinks cupboard.
Ice bucket, dirty glasses and dishes from round table.

RE–SET

Lighter from coffee table to c. of back radiator shelf.
Open u.s. window.
Close curtains.
Bedroom door closed.
c. door open.
Tidy cushions.
To original place:
Telephone book from under drinks cupboard.
Telephone from sofa table.
Stool with records.
Cigarette box and matches from top shelf sofa table.
Off R. *in kitchen:*
Two champagne glasses. (JIMMY.)
Bottle of champagne. (JIMMY.)
Pump and cork for noise of cork.
Mug of water. (JANE.)
Two glasses of water. (JANE.)
Kettle. (JIMMY.)
Hot water bottle. (JIMMY.)
Jug of water for filling hot water bottle.

Standing by for scene change:

False top set with clean tablecloth.

> *First place:* knife, fork, and small knife. Cup, saucer, and teaspoon.
> Side plate, and napkin. Two invitations in envelopes.
> *Second place:* knife, fork, and small knife. Cup, saucer, and teaspoon.
> Side plate, and napkin. Business letters. *Express* and *The Times.*
> *Third place:* knife, fork, and small knife. Cup, saucer, and teaspoon.
> Side plate, and napkin. Two letters.

Trolley set with:

> Two plates.
> Coffee pot, and milk jug.
> Eggs (scrambled) in dish.
> Spoon, and fork to serve.

PERSONAL

> DAVID:
>> Latch key on ring.
>> Jane's evening bag.

ACT II Scene 2

STRIKE

> Tray from table in window.
> Glass and biscuit tin from coffee table.
> Glass from sofa table.
> Glass from near telephone.
> Sheila's evening wrap from chair D.R.C.
> Sheila's evening bag from back radiator shelf.
> Small dirty ashtray from sofa table.
> Champagne bottle from coffee table.

RE-SET

> Round table to Act I Scene 1 marks.
> Chairs round it as in Act I, Scene 1.

SET

> False top on round table.
> Wastepaper basket by U.S. arm of sofa.
> Dispatch case in chair U.R.
> Flowers on back of sofa.
> Clean, large unbreakable ashtray on sofa table.
> Open curtains.
> Open D.S. window.
> Tidy cushions.
> Doors closed.

Off c. *in hall:*

> Bouquet of flowers. (DAVID.)
> Umbrella and hat. (JIMMY.)

WARDROBE

SHEILA

Act I

Sc. 1. Blue woollen day dress (blue kid shoes).
Sc. 2. Floral silk house coat (white kid shoes).
Yellow taffeta evening gown (shoes and bag to match).

Act II

Sc. 1. Yellow dress as above with purple velvet cloak.
Sc. 2. Blue and yellow silk dressing gown (blue sandals).
Dark grey day dress (black suede shoes).
(Diamond necklace. Brooch, bracelet and ring.)

MABEL

Act I

Sc. 2. Mole brown cocktail dress trimmed with sequins.
Loose coat to match lined pink (ear-rings).
Sequin hat—bag. Shoes to match.

JANE

Act I

Sc. 1. White and green spot dressing gown (blue velvet slippers).
Sc. 2. White embroidered Anglais evening dress (mauve satin slippers).

Act II

Sc. 1. Dress as above with wrap and bag. Gloves.
Sc. 2. Green silk dress (beige kid shoes).

CLARISSA

Act I

Sc. 2. Blue and mauve tulle evening dress. Bag, slippers and gloves.

JIMMY

Act I

Sc. 1. Blue lounge suit.
Dressing gown.
Sc. 2. Evening dress tails.

Act II

Sc. 1. Evening dress tails.
Sc. 2. Pyjama trousers and slippers.
Grey lounge suit.

DAVID HOYLAKE-JOHNSTON

Act I

Sc. 2. Evening dress tails.

Act II

Sc. 1. Evening dress tails.
Sc. 2. Lounge suit.

DAVID BULLOCH

Act I

Sc. 2. Evening dress tails.

Act II

Sc. 2. Guards uniform (complete, officer's).

MRS. EDGAR   Maid.